An Apology for Apologetics

FAITH MEETS FAITH

An Orbis Series in Interreligious Dialogue

Paul F. Knitter, General Editor

In our contemporary world, the many religions and spiritualities stand in need of greater intercommunication and cooperation. More than ever before, they must speak to, learn from, and work with each other, in order to maintain their own identity and vitality and so to contribute to fashioning a better world.

FAITH MEETS FAITH seeks to promote interreligious dialogue by providing an open forum for the exchanges between and among followers of different religious paths. While the series wants to encourage creative and bold responses to the new questions of pluralism confronting religious persons today, it also recognizes the present plurality of perspectives concerning the methods and content of interreligious dialogue.

This series, therefore, does not want to endorse any one school of thought. By making available to both the scholarly community and the general public works that represent a variety of religious and methodological viewpoints, FAITH MEETS FAITH hopes to foster and focus the emerging encounter among the religions of the world.

Already published:

FAITH MEETS FAITH SERIES

An Apology for Apologetics

A Study in the Logic of Interreligious Dialogue

Paul J. Griffiths

ORBIS BOOKS

Maryknoll, New York 10545

The Catholic Foreign Mission Society of America (Maryknoll) recruits and trains people for overseas missionary service. Through Orbis Books, Maryknoll aims to foster the international dialogue that is essential to mission. The books published, however, reflect the opinions of their authors and are not meant to represent the official position of the society.

Library of Congress Cataloging-in-Publication Data

Griffiths, Paul J.
    An apology for apologetics : a study in the logic of interreligious
dialogue / Paul J. Griffiths.
      p.   cm. — (Faith meets faith series)
    Includes bibliographical references
    ISBN 0-88344-762-2 — ISBN 0-88344-761-4 (pbk.)
    1. Religions — Relations. 2. Apologetics. I. Title. II. Series:
Faith meets faith.
BL410.G75   1991   91-15134
291.2 — dc20   CIP

This book is for my mother, Pat Griffiths

From the age of fifteen, dogma has been the fundamental principle of my religion: I know no other religion; I cannot enter into the idea of any other sort of religion; religion, as a mere sentiment, is to me a dream and a mockery. As well can there be filial love without the fact of a father, as devotion without the fact of a Supreme Being.

J. H. Newman, *Apologia*, chapter 2

yato vinā dharmapravicayena nâsti kleśôpaśamâbhyupāyah kleśāś ca lokaṃ bhramayanti saṃsāramahārṇave 'smin atas tad dhetos tasya dharmapravicayasyârthe śāstrā kila buddhenâbhidharma uktaḥ/ na hi vinā abhidharmôpadeśena śiṣyaḥ śakto dharmān pravicetum iti/

Vasubandhu, *Abhidharmakośabhāṣya*, I.3

Contents

Preface

In this short book I defend the need for the traditional discipline of apologetics as one important component of interreligious dialogue. The book is of a genre now almost entirely démodé in the academic world: it is a short polemical work, written with a nonspecialist audience in mind, and concerned with an issue of pressing contemporary interest. It is, I think, short enough to be read through in a day, and is intended to be sufficiently free of the jargon of philosophers and theologians to be capable of being understood by any literate and interested individual. And it is intended also to exemplify the virtues for which it argues, since it is itself a polemical work written in defense of a particular position and as a refutation of those that seem incompatible with its thesis. The goal of a book such as this is to stimulate debate; if it succeeds in doing so, it will have achieved its aims. The correctness of the position argued for is secondary.

Who should be interested? All members of any religious communities who take seriously the implications of their membership, and are concerned with how to think about those whose religious convictions and practices seem to differ significantly from their own. Also, anyone concerned about the functions and implications of the convictions of religious communities in international affairs should find much here of use: to see that engagement in apologetics in the sense argued for in this book is required for religious communities in some settings is to begin to understand, among many other things, why some British Muslims feel impelled to burn anti-Islamic books in Bradford, why some Buddhist monks in Sri Lanka feel called upon to foster and encourage anti-Tamil violence, and why some conservative Catholic Christians in the United States of America are willing to bomb clinics in which advice on abortion is given to pregnant women.

This book is directed against an underlying scholarly orthodoxy on the goals and functions of interreligious dialogue. This orthodoxy suggests that understanding is the only legitimate goal; that judgement and criticism of religious beliefs or practices other than those of one's own community is always inappropriate; and that an active defense of the truth of those beliefs and practices to which one's community appears committed is always to be shunned. I explore some reasons for the popularity of this position in contemporary Western theological academies in the book that follows; I also offer arguments against it. I try to show that such an orthodoxy (which tends to include the view that the very idea of orthodoxy has no sense) produces a discourse that is pallid, platitudinous, and degutted. Its products are intellectual pacifiers for the immature: pleasant to suck on but not very nourishing.

I have decided not to burden the text with explanatory notes and documentation of sources. The positions I analyze and argue against in the book are, for the most part, treated simply as abstract possibilities, set forth as such, and criticized as such. I am interested in them primarily from the systematic viewpoint, not from the historical or exegetical. In almost every case, though, the positions discussed, or some approximation to them, are actually held and argued for by some individual (or, more usually, by some group). My discussions of these positions are always indebted, more or less heavily, to the work of scholars who have trodden this ground before me. I have noted these debts and made some suggestions for further reading in a short bibliographical essay appended to the main text. The suggestions made in that essay are not, however, intended as anything approaching a full documentation of the state of play on any of the issues discussed.

I have some specific debts to be acknowledged here: to Phil Quinn, who (though he is probably not aware of it) has provided me with a model of how to think philosophically about religion; to William A. Christian, Sr., whose books have been an inspiration though I have never met him; to the faculty and staff of the department of theology at the University of Notre Dame, and most especially to Joseph Wawrykow, David Burrell, and James T. Burtchaell, each of whom has been both mentor and friend; to the participants in the University of Chicago Divinity School's colloquia on "Religions in History and Culture" from 1986–89, and most especially to Frank Reynolds, the originator and director of those colloquia; to the priests and people of the Cathedral of St. James in South Bend, Indiana, and most especially to Jeffrey Lee, who has helped me to understand something of what it means to practice Christianity; to Peg Harker, who read the whole book in manuscript and gave me many useful suggestions; to Del Lewis, with whom I first discussed some of the thoughts presented here and who has graciously given me permission to use some of his own words contained in articles that we wrote together several years ago; and finally to Judith Heyhoe, who has always encouraged me and who gave me special support and love during the writing of this book.

1

The Necessity of Interreligious Apologetics

1.1 THE PRINCIPLE OF THE NECESSITY OF INTERRELIGIOUS APOLOGETICS

In this chapter I shall state the basic principle for which this work is concerned to argue, and shall clarify its terms. I call this principle the *necessity of interreligious apologetics* (the NOIA principle). It is concerned, conceptually, to show how religious communities should relate themselves to one another. More exactly, the NOIA principle is concerned with one important dimension of the epistemic and ethical duties of those who act as spokespersons and formulators of doctrine for religious communities. It argues, briefly, that such spokespersons should, if and when certain circumstances obtain, relate themselves apologetically to claims made by their opposite numbers within other religious communities. I make this argument as a Christian thinker, from within a perspective conditioned by Christian faith. But if the arguments presented here are good, I expect the NOIA principle to apply to all (or almost all) religious communities.

As will become apparent, the NOIA principle is not uncontroversial; it offends, if taken seriously, against many (perhaps most) of the theological orthodoxies of our time, including the orthodoxy that the very idea of orthodoxy has no sense. It should, if acted upon, have important practical effects both upon the ways in which religious intellectuals typically think about the claims to truth espoused by their own communities, and upon the ways in which they typically think about the claims to truth expressed by other communities.

In subsequent chapters I shall explore the main reasons why the NOIA principle offends against so many current intellectual perspectives, and shall canvass the main objections to it; here, my concern is simply to state the principle and to clarify its major terms. It may nevertheless be of some use at this point to explain why it is important to argue for the necessity of apologetics as one dimension of a religiously proper response to the much-discussed issue of religious pluralism.

It has become a truism, though none the less true for that, to say that the world has grown smaller; that the community within which each of us lives is no longer the church or the nation, but the world; and that Christian theology as an intellectual discipline (or indeed any other kind of theology) cannot legitimately be done without making the realization of these things central to its practice. Those who say this the loudest are, however, often the last to offer a serious treatment of the pressing intellectual problems that such a realization brings. How is systematic theology to be practised if the tradition-based norms that have shaped it are placed in and relativized by a context of radical religious pluralism? What is the status and validity of Christian ethical and metaethical theory in such a context? What, in such a context, can the adjective "Christian" mean? Is it genuinely possible to engage in constructive theological thought comparatively?

Among these large questions that of the nature and status of interreligious apologetics is significant, partly because it is, at the moment, so widely ignored. "Apologetics" has itself become a term laden with negative connotations: to be an apologist for the truth of one religious claim or set of claims over against another is, in certain circles, seen as not far short of being a racist. And the term has passed into popular currency, to the extent that it has, as a simple label for argument in the service of a predetermined orthodoxy, argument concerned not to demonstrate but to convince, and, if conviction should fail, to browbeat into submission.

In almost all mainstream institutions in which theology is taught in the USA and in Europe, apologetics as an intellectual discipline does not figure prominently in the curriculum. You will look for it in vain in the catalogues of the Divinity Schools at Harvard or Chicago; liberal Protestants have never been wedded to the practice of interreligious apologetics, and while the Roman Catholic Church has a long and honorable tradition of apologetics, interreligious and other, its approach to theological thinking about non-Christian religious communities has moved far from the apologetical since the Second Vatican Council, and especially since the promulgation of the conciliar document *Nostra Aetate*. Why then choose to devote even such a short work as this to a topic that appears theologically dead outside all but the most conservative and sectarian religious communities?

A detailed justification of the choice is in the work that follows. As a preliminary defense I can at this point only say that a proper understanding of the status and importance of interreligious apologetics is essential to a clarification of the significance of religious claims to truth made in a context of radical religious pluralism. Religious claims to truth are typically absolute claims: claims to explain everything; claims about the universal rightness and applicability of a certain set of values together with the ways of life that embody and perpetuate them; and claims whose referent possesses maximal greatness. These tendencies to absoluteness, although they have certainly been typical of Christian doctrines, are not typical only of them; they are characteristic also of many of the most interesting claims made by the religious virtuosi of non-Christian traditions. Examples will be adduced in the course of this study. It is just this tendency to absoluteness that makes religious truth-claims of such interest and gives them such power; to ignore it is to eviscerate them, to do them the disservice of making them other than what they take themselves to be. Apologetics, as I shall define and defend it, is thus an essential component of interreligious relations, though it is by no means the whole story. It is for these reasons, and for others that will become apparent as this work proceeds, that I judge it so important to offer a defense of interreligious apologetics.

The NOIA principle, stated formally, is an if-then conditional. It affirms, that is, that if a given state of affairs obtains, a certain course of action should follow:

> If representative intellectuals belonging to some specific religious community come to judge at a particular time that some or all of their own doctrine-expressing sentences are incompatible with some alien religious claim(s), then they should feel obliged to engage in both positive and negative apologetics vis-à-vis these alien religious claim(s) and their promulgators.

I shall argue not only that when the antecedent obtains the conclusion follows, that when representative intellectuals of religious communities find themselves in the situation described, they should engage in apologetics; but also that, in at least some cases, the antecedent does obtain, that representative intellectuals do sometimes find themselves in just such a situation. Some of the terms used in this abstract statement of the NOIA principle have a more or less technical sense, and it will be useful to clarify their meaning at this point in the enterprise.

1.2 RELIGIOUS COMMUNITIES AND THEIR REPRESENTATIVE INTELLECTUALS

Religious communities are difficult to define and demarcate. Formally, I shall consider a religious community to be any group of persons that would, severally and collectively, acknowledge themselves to be members of some community that is recognizably religious. This, like all formal definitions, sounds elegant and is not of much use. It says nothing about the key substantive question of what makes a given community religious, and offers no help in resolving issues of demarcation and membership. There are reasons, though, why it is difficult to do better, and it is worth offering some brief comments on them.

First, there is the difficult question of what a religious community is and how membership in it is constituted. In one sense religious communities are entities available for empirical inspection: one can go and look at a group of Anglican Christians gathered on a Sunday morning for eucharist and rightly judge that one is looking at a religious community engaged in one of its idiosyncratic activities. Or one can go and observe a group of Theravada Buddhist monks in Sri Lanka engaged in public recitation of the *pratimoksha*, a summary of the rules of monastic discipline, and rightly come to the same conclusion. Or one can observe the ecstatic speaking in tongues that occurs at a gathering of charismatic Christians, or the creation of a *mandala* in colored sand by Tibetan Buddhist monks, accompanied by ritual chant and action. Examples could easily be multiplied.

But the fact that religious communities and their actions are available for empirical study does not provide an easy answer to the abstract questions of what they are, how membership in them is constituted, and how their representative intellectuals are typically related to them. Let us consider two of the examples mentioned: that of the Anglican Christians gathered for celebration of the eucharist, and that of the Theravada Buddhists gathered to publicly recite the *pratimoksha*. In both cases the community is constituted on a number of different levels. First, there is the most basic level: our first community is Christian and our second Buddhist. But this is not very helpful. Multicultural polyglot entities such as "Buddhism" and "Christianity" are semifictional; they have, to the historian's eye, no essential properties other, perhaps, than the very abstract one of being historically related in some more or less tenuous fashion in the one case to the historical individual Jesus of Nazareth, and in the other to the historical individual whose name we do not certainly know, but who has come to be dignified with the title of Shakyamuni Buddha, the Awakened One, the Sage of the Shakyas.

Both our Anglican Christians and our Theravada Buddhists meet this criterion, but so do many others who may hold in common with our examples nothing in the way of doctrine, practice, or institutional forms. The poet Allan Ginsberg, for example, is fond of calling himself a Buddhist, and has been connected for some time with the attempt to transplant a particular Tibetan Buddhist lineage to the United States of America associated with the name of the late Chogyam Trungpa. But he would probably feel little attraction toward the very traditional and highly ordered monastic life of a conservative Theravadin monk, and might find no set of claims to truth upon which he and such a Theravadin could agree. Similarly, the amount of common ground in doctrine, practice, or institutional forms between a high church Anglican and, say, a fervent Christian Scientist is vanishingly small.

This is not to deny that both Ginsberg and our traditionally minded Theravadin are Buddhist in some sense; or that both Anglicans and the followers of Mary Baker Eddy are Christian. One can arrive at such a denial only by constructing a normative rather than a descriptive reading of the Christian (or the Buddhist) tradition. A normative definition of a community is one that sets up norms, either of doctrine or practice, to which persons must adhere in order to be considered members of that community. Its purpose is to exclude some and include others, to set up conditions that must be met in order for membership in the community to occur and be maintained. So, for example, it might be claimed that one must consume the body and blood of Jesus Christ through the ceremony of the eucharist at least three times a year in order to be considered Christian; or that one must consider a certain set of texts in the Pali language as the exclusive sacred and authoritative word of the Buddha in order to merit the title "Buddhist." On these normative readings of the Buddhist and Christian communities it is unlikely that either Ginsberg is a Buddhist or that Christian Scientists merit the adjective in their name.

Such normatively exclusivist readings of semifictional entities like "Christianity" and "Buddhism" (not to mention "Islam," "Hinduism," and "Judaism") are, of course, commonly constructed, usually with the goal of affirming the membership of constructors and denying that of those who do not agree with them in some important particulars. I do not wish to argue here either that such normative readings should be constructed or that they should not; I wish only to point out that no such reading can be constructed on a historical basis, that no institutional forms are found that operate within and are relevant to every member of the semifictional entities under consideration here, and that this most basic level of membership in a religious community will therefore not be of much importance for the argument contained in this work. I shall thus not be much concerned in what follows with whether a particular group is "Buddhist" or "Christian" or "Muslim" or whatever. Apologetical discourse does not operate at this level of generality (even though it may often claim to and in its surface discourse appear as if it did), and anyone who claims to be a spokesperson for Christians or Buddhists is in fact acting as a spokesperson for some subgroup within these large amorphous groupings. It is these subgroups and their constituents that I shall usually intend when I speak of "religious communities," even though I shall often, out of necessity, use locutions such as "Christian" and "Buddhist."

A caveat is in order at this point. I do not intend to claim by what has been said in the immediately preceding paragraphs that normative and exclusivist definitions of Christianity or Buddhism are improper or useless. In certain contexts they are essential, and I frequently make use of them myself in such contexts. If, for example, it seemed important for polemical purposes, or in the interests of drawing attention to some significant elements within the complex of historical events that constitute the Christian tradition, to argue that no one who advocates genocide as a significant instrument of foreign policy can properly claim to belong to a Christian community, I would not hesitate to do so. But I do not have such purposes in mind here, and will therefore be concerned in what follows with religious communities in a less amorphous and more specific sense.

I am dealing, then, with specific religious communities, not with global semifictional entities. But even here there are no universally applicable guidelines to be used in demarcating a community. Some communities have well-defined requirements for entry and maintenance of membership, but many do not. In the case of Anglican Christians, entry requirements would include baptism and sometimes confirmation, while maintenance requirements would theoretically include regular church attendance, twice yearly communion, and some level of financial support by donation to the local parish. For a lay Theravada Buddhist, entry requirements would include a ritual taking of the three refuges through the triple formula "I take refuge in the Buddha, I take refuge in the doctrine, I take refuge in the monastic community," and maintenance requirements would include (theoretically and among other things) an ordering of one's life to harmonize with the ethical proscriptions enshrined in the pan-Buddhist ethical code known as the five precepts, and the continuation of a proper relationship (usually through donation) to the monastic community.

But who is to say how, precisely, membership in some of the radically individualistic antihierarchical Protestant Christian groups is determined? Does one, for instance, qualify as part of the Christian community shaped by Jimmy Swaggart's television ministry if one tunes in to the broadcasts now and then and sends an occasional donation? Is one a Gelukpa Buddhist if one attends a weekly *puja* service in Madison, Wisconsin, and receives teachings (in English), expounding the philosophical implications of the teachings of Tsong-kha-pa, the Tibetan founder of this Buddhist lineage? There are no obvious answers to these questions.

More difficult still is the question of what religion is, and of what it is about a particular community's behavior and beliefs that makes it religious. Religion, like pornography, is something recognizable (usually) but impossibly difficult to define or even delineate. Fortunately, since all the examples drawn on for the purposes of this study will come from one or other of the five historical complexes of events, beliefs, practices, and institutions that are often called "world religions" (Christianity, Judaism, Hinduism, Islam, and Buddhism—most will be drawn from the first and last in this list), I can conveniently use the term "religion" to refer to what has gone on and what now goes on within the borders of those complexes, semifictional though they are, and leave matters there.

To return to the formal definition of the NOIA principle offered at the beginning of this section and bearing in mind the comments just made: a religious community is, for the purposes of this study, any specific group of persons who, severally or collectively, bear a historical relationship that they take to be of salvific significance to one or another of those streams of events called "world religions."

The first clause of the NOIA principle introduced the idea that religious communities, in the sense given, may have "representative intellectuals" connected with them. A little more needs to be said about this. Briefly, a representative intellectual of a specific religious community is one who makes pronouncements, either oral or written, on matters of doctrine or practice, pronouncements that are taken to be authoritative by nonintellectual members of the community. So, the pronouncements of the Dalai Lama, both written and spoken, are authoritative for most Tibetan Buddhists (and thus most Tibetans), but especially for Gelukpa monastics. The pronouncements of the pope are authoritative for most Roman Catholics; and those of the Archbishop of Canterbury for most members of the Anglican communion.

These are examples of representative intellectuals who speak for religious communities broader than specific local groups. They do so in virtue of the fact that their religious communities have a well-developed and thoroughly institutionalized hierarchical authority structure, a structure that both allows for and requires the handing down of pronouncements on matters of doctrine and practice that are theoretically binding upon all those specific local communities affiliated with it. Reality, of course, usually does not match theory in such hierarchically structured communities. Rather few American Roman Catholics, for instance, seem to feel bound by pronouncements from authority figures in the Vatican on the proper uses of reproductive technology. Nevertheless, such communities have easily recognizable representative intellectuals, men (usually) whose authoritative statements as to what the community should believe and practice are frequently available in oppressively detailed and lengthy written documents.

But there are, of course, religious communities lacking this kind of hierarchical structure, communities whose representative intellectuals, if recognizable at all, are visible only at a much more local level. Such, for instance, is the Theravada Buddhist monastic community, and such also are some of the more extreme antiauthoritarian Protestant Christian groups (Anabaptists, Mennonites, Amish, and so forth). This is not to say that such groups have no representative intellectuals; only that their place within such communities differs institutionally from that of representative intellectuals in more hierarchically ordered communities. There are, for example, many intellectual Theravada Buddhist monks, writers of books and articulators of particular doctrinal perspectives, whose works are, in various complex ways, "representative" of and authoritative for the monastic community in a larger sense. There are also, in a more localized sense, specific monks in specific village communities who act as representative intellectuals for the lay Buddhists in those communities. These local representative intellectuals rather rarely write books or function in any public sphere broader than the village, but their functions overlap in large part with those of representative intellectuals as I am using the term.

There are, finally, religious communities that self-consciously repudiate the very idea of intellectuals representing their views. This is usually for one of two reasons. Either the communities in question are radically egalitarian and wish to disavow the hierarchical implications of allowing intellectuals to represent the views of nonintellectual members; or they may be ideologically (and perhaps therefore also oxymoronically) anti-intellectual. Instances of the first type might include some basic Christian communities or house churches, very small groups, usually not more than twenty or so in membership, whose sole purpose is the fostering of egalitarian community life, and who thus tend not to have or need (or at least to say that they neither have nor need) representative intellectuals to formulate the views of the community. Instances of the second type might include ideologically anti-intellectual Zen Buddhists, who tend to claim that the sole purpose of the religious life is the transcendence of the dichotomizing activities of the intellect.

I suspect, however, that both the radically egalitarian and the radically anti-intellectual religious communities do in practice produce representative intellectuals to develop and articulate coherent doctrinal positions. The egalitarian communal life of the basic Christian communities turns out to have significant politico-economic implications for the larger societies within which it is lived, and these implications tend, quite properly, to get voiced. They have been voiced in Latin America, among other places, during the last two decades by those who have come to be known as liberation theologians. These intellectuals are to a large extent best understood as the representative intellectuals of the basic Christian communities. Even iconoclastic and anti-intellectual Zen Buddhists find it difficult to do without representative intellectuals: the position that all doctrinal views are false is itself a doctrinal view, and needs to be argued with considerable sophistication (as indeed it is by Zen Buddhists) if it is to carry conviction. Hence the need for representative intellectuals, even for anti-intellectual religious communities.

It may seem as though my stress on the significance of representative intellectuals is itself elitist and antiegalitarian; to some, perhaps, it may even appear fundamentally irreligious. Have not all persons a right to articulate their own religious opinions, and a right to do so without bowing to the dictates of professional theologians? Why not extend, then, the normative "should" of the NOIA principle (". . . they should feel obliged to engage in both positive and negative apologetics vis-à-vis these alien religious claim(s) . . .") to all religious persons? While I would certainly not wish to deny the religious rights of all, and while I hope to avoid the still more egregious error of identifying the complex phenomenon of being religious with the doctrinal formulations that govern some dimensions of it, there still seem to be benefits in restricting the NOIA principle's application to the belief-forming and belief-maintenance practices of representative intellectuals.

First, there is the obvious fact that most religious persons have little interest in and less understanding of the doctrine-expressing sentences of the religious communities to which they belong. It would put too great a burden upon their belief-forming and belief-maintenance practices to require that they engage in apologetics every time they encounter a threatening alien religious claim. Second, the formulation of the NOIA principle, while certainly directed at representative intellectuals, in no way rules out the engagement of others in the activities recommended by it, nor even discourages such engagement.

I shall assume, then, for the purposes of this study, that all or almost all religious communities have representative intellectuals among their members, and that the major function of these intellectuals is to interpret the data of the tradition to its nonintellectual members, and, above all else, to formulate and articulate doctrine (I shall say more in a moment about what doctrine is). The NOIA principle is directed at these groups of intellectuals. It is a principle that governs their discursive practices, a principle that tells them how to think about and how to argue for the doctrines of their community in a certain kind of situation. It is to this situation, the situation envisaged by the NOIA principle, that I now turn.

1.3 DOCTRINE-EXPRESSING SENTENCES

The NOIA principle makes use of the term "doctrine-expressing sentences." By this I mean sentences in some natural language (whatever the language of the community happens to be), which are taken by the community either to make or to entail claims about the nature of things, or claims about the value of certain courses of action; these sentences must also be regarded by the community as of some significance for its religious life, and for the salvation of its members. I assume that most religious communities engage in the production of such sentences, and that even those that do not, nevertheless demonstrate their implicit assent to some set of doctrine-expressing sentences by what they say and do.

To illustrate: the sacred texts of the Theravada Buddhist communities contain a large number of sentences in Pali, a natural language, even though not one that is any longer anyone's mother tongue. What is explicitly said in these sentences (and, therefore, what is entailed by what is explicitly said) is taken by the representative intellectuals of those communities to be both true and of great salvific significance. Further, the sentences formulated by contemporary intellectuals representing the Theravada Buddhist communities, often in expounding and commenting upon those contained in the sacred texts, are also, though in somewhat different ways, taken to be authoritative for such communities. So it is possible to find, without too much difficulty, sentences formulated by the representative intellectuals of these Buddhist communities that make claims about the nature of things.

It is frequently said, for instance, that every existent is transient; sometimes, with more precision, that every existent is strictly momentary; often that there is a set of necessary and sufficient conditions for the occurrence of any event whatever. It is also often claimed that personal proper names, such as Devadatta (the Indian equivalent of John Doe), while certainly capable of being used in all the usual conventional ways, refer to nothing. They label, that is to say, no substance, no possessor of properties, which can properly be designated by such linguistic items as "Devadatta." And so forth.

Claims of this sort may appear to be rarefied, abstract, and thoroughly philosophical, and it may be far from obvious at first sight how assent to them could be taken by the members of any religious community to be of salvific significance. To demonstrate that these doctrine-expressing sentences are so understood by many Buddhists would require a full-scale excursion into the exegesis of the Theravada tradition. That is not my purpose here, and the assertion that these sentences are indeed taken to be salvifically significant will have to be accepted on trust (though something more will be said about it in chapter 6), as will many of the historical assertions made in the course of this study.

But something should be said as to the ways in which such assertions are thought to have salvific significance. Briefly, it is important to assent to the claim that all existents are impermanent and that personal proper names refer to nothing enduring, because these beliefs (together with other collateral beliefs and entailments) are instrumental in fostering, for the individual who holds them, the basic Buddhist virtue of reducing passionate attachment. If one does not believe that persons are enduring entities, then, so the argument goes, one will be less passionately attached to them, less likely to organize one's life around a basic and avoidable cognitive error.

This Buddhist example illustrates splendidly a convenient way of classifying doctrine-expressing sentences: I shall assume that these are either descriptive claims about the nature of things, or assertions of value. Of the former kind are such doctrine-expressing sentences as the Qur'anic *there is no God but God and Muhammad is his prophet*; of the latter kind are such doctrine-expressing sentences as *you should love the Lord your God with all your heart, all your mind, and all your soul*. The former makes a claim about what exists and the nature of what exists; the latter recommends, or even demands, that a certain course of action be undertaken, with the suggestion (sometimes explicit but usually implicit) that the course of action in question is valuable—perhaps supremely valuable. I do not claim that this way of classifying doctrine-expressing sentences is the only way, nor even that it will account for all of them (though I rather suspect that it will). I make use of this classification and analysis for heuristic purposes only.

I also assume that doctrine-expressing sentences of both kinds are capable of being true or false (which is not the same thing as claiming that knowledge of their truth or falsity is available to me, or to anyone). This is perhaps more obvious for descriptive claims about the nature of things than for assertions of value. But even in the latter case, in which doctrine-expressing sentences are often sentences framed in the optative or imperative moods, it should not be difficult to see that the assertions of value that necessarily underly such commands or pious hopes can be true or false. If, for example, I tell you to engage in ceaseless recollection of the Buddha, and if I further claim this as a doctrine-expressing sentence of my religious community, this is presumably because I judge the sentence *it is desirable that you engage in ceaseless recollection of the Buddha*, or perhaps even the sentence *it is desirable that everyone engages in ceaseless recollection of the Buddha*, to be true. So, mutatis mutandis, for claims such as *sell all you have and give to the poor*.

In fact, the assumption that doctrine-expressing sentences can be true (or false) is itself parasitic upon a number of other assumptions. Specifically, it is associated with a propositional view of truth which, in its usual form, sees propositions as the sole bearers of truth or falsity, and natural-language sentences as being capable of expressing propositions. This propositional view also sees belief as an attitude that persons (or communities) have toward propositions. To say *I believe that P*, where *P* is a proposition-expressing sentence in some natural language — such as, for example, the English sentence *there is one God, creator of heaven and earth* — is to say at least that I assent to the truth of the proposition expressed by that sentence. This propositional view is not unproblematic; I shall canvass some of the more important objections to it in the sphere of philosophical theology in the chapters that follow. At this point I simply note that the propositional view, or something very much like it, of the truth and falsity of doctrine-expressing sentences is presupposed by the NOIA principle.

It may be wondered why, if I am presupposing a propositional view of truth and belief, I have chosen to speak in the NOIA principle not of propositions but rather of doctrine-expressing *sentences*. The reason is simple: natural-language sentences are all that the representative intellectuals of one community have access to when studying the doctrines of a religious community other than their own. Suppose a Hasidic Jew wants to know what a member of the Soka Gakkai really believes about the Jewish people. He has no recourse other than the writings or oral statements of Soka Gakkai members, and these in turn consist of natural-language sentences. The natural language in this case will of course be Japanese, with which I suspect rather few Hasidic Jews are familiar; but this has no bearing upon the theoretical point.

Before I leave the topic of doctrine-expressing sentences, another relatively minor issue needs to be mentioned. For any religious community, the set of its doctrine-expressing sentences will not be coextensive with the set of sentences to which its members give assent. This is for obvious reasons: presumably most American members of religious communities would assent to the sentence *Michael Jordan was one of the ten best players in the NBA in 1989*, but rather few (save for those for whom the Chicago Bulls are of ultimate significance) would want to claim this sentence as a doctrine-expressing sentence of the community, simply because it is of no salvific significance and has no clear functions within the religious life of any religious community. I reiterate, then, that a doctrine-expressing sentence is one that is taken by a specific religious community to be of some salvific importance, or (what is not always the same thing) to be of some importance for the religious life of the community.

Doctrine-expressing sentences, then, are objects available for empirical study. It is relatively easy to find them out and to analyze them, though rather less easy to be sure that one knows what the community that formulated them means by them if one is not oneself a member of that community (and sometimes even if one is). If one wants to know what the doctrine-expressing sentences of a given religious community are, one simply has to go to the representative intellectuals of that community and ask. Many religious communities take the trouble to set down their doctrine-expressing sentences in books for the delectation of the casual reader, some enshrine them in credal formulae, chant them in ritual settings, and otherwise scatter them abroad. Given the easy availability of these fascinating objects, it is suprising that so few professional intellectuals take the trouble to study them as their formulators intended them to be understood: as complex and interesting claims to truth. But I shall return to this, too, in the chapters that follow, especially in chapter 2.

1.4 ALIEN RELIGIOUS CLAIMS

To return to the NOIA principle: I suggested in my formulation of that principle that it is possible for representative intellectuals of religious communities to come to judge that some alien religious claim(s) are not compatible with their own doctrine-expressing sentences. What, then, is an alien religious claim? Briefly, a particular claim is an alien religious claim with respect to some religious community if and only if it is a doctrine-expressing sentence of another religious community that does not express a proposition also expressed by any doctrine-expressing sentence of the religious community with respect to which it is alien.

For example: the Roman Catholic doctrine-expressing sentence *one should attend Mass frequently* is an alien religious claim with respect to, among many other examples, the community of Rissho Koseikai (one of Japan's so-called new religions) members. The Buddhist doctrine-expressing sentence *passionate attachment is to be avoided as detrimental to the practice of the religious life* is an alien religious claim with respect to the comunity of Shi'ite Muslims. And so forth. It is important to notice that the fact of a particular doctrine-expressing sentence being an alien claim with respect to some community does not by itself mean that it is unacceptable to that community or incompatible with any of its own doctrine-expressing sentences. It is at least conceivable, even if not very likely, that a group of representative Rissho Koseikai intellectuals might come to accept and promulgate the Roman Catholic doctrine-expressing sentence mentioned (in which case, of course, it would cease to be an alien claim with respect to the Rissho Koseikai), and yet not thereby dissolve them-selves into the Church Catholic. The fact that a given religious claim is alien to a specific religious community says only that what is expressed by it is not also a doctrine of that religious community: it is neutral with regard to acceptability. It may turn out, upon examination, that the alien claim can become a doctrine-expressing sentence of the community with respect to which it was once alien. Or this may turn out not to be possible, in which case the claim remains alien.

Given this definition of an alien religious claim, the NOIA principle envisages a situation in which some such claim is judged by representative intellectuals of some religious community to be incompatible with some one (or several) of their own doctrine-expressing sentences. What forms might such incompatibility take? I shall mostly be concerned with two types of incompatibility, types correlated with the twofold classification of doctrine-expressing sentences already given. The first kind of incompatibility is strictly logical, and might occur between two descriptive doctrine-expressing sentences. If one doctrine-expressing sentence is true, the other cannot be. For example: suppose one religious community asserts the doctrine-expressing sentence *Jesus Christ is the same yesterday, today, and forever* and another the doctrine-expressing sentence *everything that exists does so momentarily*. The prima facie incompatibility is clear enough to need little comment. Of course, the appearance of incompatibility of this direct and irreconcilable kind is not the same as its reality; it is often the case, as I shall show, that two assertions that appear to be incompatible when con-sidered in isolation turn out not to be so when considered in the broader context of the conceptual system that gives them meaning. But there seems to be no pressing reason to assume that such direct incompatibility never occurs or cannot occur.

The second kind of incompatibility that I have in mind is practical, and is related to those doctrine-expressing sentences that prescribe (or pro-scribe) a certain course of action, and thus express a value. Suppose one religious community enshrines among its doctrine-expressing sentences the recommendation that one should be ceaselessly mindful of God. And sup-pose a member of that religious community learns that there is an alien religious claim (that is, a doctrine-expressing sentence of another religious community) that recommends the ceaseless chanting of an invocation to the Buddha. Such a person might well conclude, not unreasonably, that these two injunctions are practically incompatible just because it is not possible for one and the same individual to carry them both out. The chain of reasoning that might lead to such a conclusion would presumably include the judgments that being mindful of God and chanting an invocation to the Buddha are not the same thing; and that one cannot do both at once. Anyone who came to such a conclusion might justifiably be accused of excessive literal-mindedness, of not being sensitive to the hyperbole so often employed in doctrine-expressing sentences. Such might indeed turn out to be the case, but it is, at least, not obviously so. It should be noted in this connection that the NOIA principle requires not that there actually be incompatibility between a doctrine-expressing sentence and an alien religious claim, but only that some representative intellectuals of some religious community should come to judge that there is. Such interpretive concerns as the question of sensitivity to hyperbole will thus often be resolved in and through the apologetical enterprise, and need not be decided in advance.

It should now be clearer what representative intellectuals of religious communities are, what doctrine-expressing sentences are, and how they may be incompatible one with another (recall that what is an alien claim with respect to one community will by definition be a doctrine-expressing sentence with respect to another). What then is apologetical discourse, and in what sense is it proper to say that religious intellectuals have a duty to engage in it?

1.5 INTERRELIGIOUS APOLOGETICS AS A DUTY

Apologetics I take to be a kind of discourse, a way of arguing with a particular aim in view, traditionally engaged in by the representative intellectuals of religious communities. It is an occasional and usually polemical discourse that operates in two quite distinctive modalities. The first is negative: in this mode, apologetical discourse is designed to show that a given critique of (any one of) the central truth-claims expressed by an ordered set of doctrine-expressing sentences fails, or that a critique of the set as a whole (as to, say, its consistence or coherence) does the same. Suppose that someone from outside the Buddhist tradition presents an argument purporting to show that two key doctrine-expressing sentences from within the tradition — say, the claim *there are no spiritual substances* and the claim *each person is reborn many times* — issue in a contradiction if taken together. A Buddhist defender of the faith will usually try to mend fences by showing that no such contradiction results, or that some important misunderstanding of the sentences in question has occurred. This is negative apologetics in action. Standard-issue Christian responses to the problem of evil, attempting to show that there is no incompatibility between sentences, such as *there is an omnipotent, omniscient, omnibenevolent God* and *there is a lot of evil in the world*, tend to be of the same logical kind.

Positive apologetics is both more complex and more interesting: it is a discourse designed to show that the ordered set of doctrine-expressing sentences constituting a particular religious community's doctrines is cognitively superior, in some important respect(s), to that constituting another religious community's doctrines. Where negative apologetics is defensive, positive apologetics is offensive; where negative apologetics mans the barricades, positive apologetics takes the battle to the enemy's camp. Positive apologetics is, by its very nature, part of an evidentialist program; it tries to show, by cumulative-case arguments, that the conceptual system it is attempting to establish is more likely than not, or more likely than some specific competitor, to be true, both in its parts and as a whole. It may also, though more rarely, try to provide a knockdown drag-out argument for the truth of one particular doctrine-expressing sentence, the kind of argument whose force one cannot preserve sanity and deny. Of this genre are some versions of the ontological argument for God's existence.

I have suggested that both kinds of apologetic are (or should be) occasional and polemical. I mean by this that they are typically occasioned by a specific challenge of some kind, or by awareness that the ordered set of sentences for which the apologia is being undertaken is not the only one in the field. This, I think, is largely the case. But it is also worth noting that, at particular points in the history of various traditions, there has been a tendency for apologetics to lose its occasional and polemical thrust and to harden into a formalistic intellectual discourse, an exercise aimed at showing that a particular set of doctrine-expressing sentences is cognitively superior to any other, even when the only competitors actually canvassed are the dry relics of long-dead intellectual systems. This was certainly often the case in Tibet, where the production of *Grub mtha'* texts was an activity of just this kind, and the same is true of many of the Roman Catholic manuals of apologetics. But this is a degenerate form of apologetics, sufficiently different in both genre and goals from the kinds of discourse I have in mind to warrant no further comment.

Apologetics also usually uses only methods of argumentation and criteria of knowledge acceptable to the adversary. This is to rule out, among other things, appeals to sources of authority not recognized by one side in the debate. A Buddhist attempt at positive apologetics vis-à-vis Christianity that does nothing other than appeal to the word of the Buddha is unlikely to be successful or fruitful in any other way. This restriction on methods of argumentation and allowable authority-sources is fully consistent with the character of apologetics as an occasional and polemical intellectual discipline, and I shall say more about it in chapter 5.

It remains to explain the thrust of the normative "should" in the NOIA principle: "[representative intellectuals of religious communities] should feel obliged to engage in both positive and negative apologetics vis-à-vis . . . alien religious claim(s) and their promulgators." I take this "should" to be, first and most interestingly, an epistemic one. That is, since religious communities characteristically assert the ordered sets of sentences that express their doctrines because they take them to be true, it is part of their epistemic duty to consider whether a challenging sentence or set of such makes it improper to continue asserting what the community asserts. This will usually initially involve engagement in some form of negative apologetics—an attempt to see whether the competing assertion fails in its claims—but it may often (and should) pass from there into positive apologetics—the attempt to show not only that the attack fails, but that the doctrines of the community under attack are cognitively superior to those of its challenger.

Secondly, the "should" in the NOIA principle is ethical in a somewhat broader sense. That is, religious communities often (though not always and not necessarily) hold that assent to sentences expressing the doctrines of the community is of some considerable salvific significance. Perhaps the strongest imaginable salvific significance that assent to some set of sentences could have is that of necessary and sufficient conditionality. Here, the relevant assent would both be necessary for the attainment of salvation (if you do not make it, you do not get it), and sufficient for that attainment (if you do make it, you will certainly get it). Very few religious communities (perhaps none) suggest that this relationship holds, and for very good reasons. Among them is the obvious fact that, if assent to any set of sentences could by itself guarantee salvation, then noncognitive attitudes, including religious practice of all kinds, would become religiously irrelevant. For example, a Buddhist intellectual who holds that assent to the three sentences *everything is impermanent, everything is unsatisfactory,* and *everything is without Self* is both necessary and sufficient for the attainment of Nirvana would also have to hold that meditational practice is not necessary for such attainment. And this would be a radically unorthodox Buddhist position. This strong position is not one that any religious community happily takes, and it scarcely warrants further consideration for the purposes of this study.

A less strong position, though still one that gives much weight to assent to sets of sentences, is that which judges the relevant relation to be one of necessary conditionality. This, I think (*pace* some of the counterpositions to be discussed), has been and remains very common in virtually all religious communities. The (pseudo)-Athanasian creed will serve as an excellent example: both in its surface logical structure (*quicunque vult . . .*) and probably in the intent of its framers, it strongly presents the position that assent to a lengthy and comparatively well-defined set of sentences is a necessary condition for the attainment of salvation.

A weaker position still is that which suggests simply that there is some kind of more or less significant positive link between assenting to some set of doctrine-expressing sentences and attaining salvation. Perhaps that the former is helpful for the latter, or that it is more helpful than any of its known competitors. This position, too, is widely instanced in all religious traditions. For theistic traditions it preserves both the importance of assent to the correct sentences, and the possibility of salvation being attained through such things as unmerited grace in default of access to the correct set of doctrine-expressing sentences.

However exactly one conceives the relation between assent to some set of doctrine-expressing sentences and the attainment of salvation, it is beyond doubt that virtually all religious communities assert that there is some such relation. Many of them also (including virtually all Christian and Buddhist communities) tend to hold that the salvation of non-members (those who, among other things, do not assent to the sentences in question) is important. The conclusion that there is an ethical imperative placed upon such communities to engage in positive apologetics is therefore at least suggested.

1.6 A BRIEF COMMENT ON SALVATION

Several times in the course of the first chapter I have used the term "salvation" and its derivatives. I have, for instance, said in 1.3 that in order for some particular natural-language sentence to qualify as a doctrine-expressing sentence of some religious community, assent to it must be regarded by the members of that community as being of salvific significance. Such locutions are not without their problems; "salvation" is, after all, an explicitly Christian term, freighted with a great deal of theological and metaphysical baggage. It might be thought that by introducing the term here I am loading the dice improperly, bringing in by subterfuge a Christian theological term that will prejudice the results of the enquiry.

It is certainly true that the traditional Christian emphasis on the necessity of salvation and the centrality of the figure of Jesus of Nazareth to its attainment has been rejected by the members of many other religious communities. Sometimes it is so rejected because it seems to locate the sphere of religious transformation altogether outside this world (one can often hear Jewish commentators on Christianity making such comments); and sometimes because of a perceived overemphasis on the person of Christ. But my use of this term is intended to introduce neither implication. I need, at this point in the enquiry, some term to refer, in a purely formal way, to the religious goal that each religious community regards as desirable for its members.

A Christian label for this is "salvation"; Buddhists might prefer Nirvana or *moksha*. But every religious community, I take it, does have some goal, purpose, or end in mind for its members. That is to say, every religious community judges that membership in it will issue in (or, perhaps, constitute) something that is qualitatively better than the other available options; and every religious community judges that assent to its doctrine-expressing sentences will serve (or, perhaps, constitute) that something. It is in this purely formal sense that I use the adjective "salvific" as it pertains to doctrine-expressing sentences. I intend no judgement at this stage, either positive or negative, as to whether the "something" in question is the same for each and every religious community.

The key terms used in the NOIA principle should now be clearer. I am claiming that there are empirically recognizable religious communities; that they usually have representative intellectuals; that these representative intellectuals typically engage, among other things, in the formulation and defense of sentences expressing doctrines of the community; that it is possible for the doctrine-expressing sentences of one community to be incompatible with those of another; and that when the representative intellectuals of a particular community judge this to be the case, they should respond apologetically.

These are not, I take it, uncontroversial claims, nor claims without pressing intellectual difficulties of their own. Many of the assumptions at work here would be rejected out of hand, for a wide variety of reasons, by influential schools of thought among both theologians and philosophers, not least by those concerned with interreligious dialogue. The following chapters deal with some of the more important among these objections.

2

The Properties of Doctrine-Expressing Sentences

Doctrine-expressing sentences are required, if the NOIA principle is ever to come into operation, to have, or at least to be capable of having, three important attributes. First, the doctrine-expressing sentences produced by the representative intellectuals of one religious community must be capable of being understood, at least in part and to some extent, by those of another religious community. If this is not the case, for theoretical or practical reasons, then clearly any judgement by the representative intellectuals of one community as to the incompatibility of their doctrine-expressing sentences with those of another community will be ill-founded and the NOIA principle will never come into operation.

Second, at least some doctrine-expressing sentences must extend the scope of their claims beyond the bounds of the community in which they are asserted. If this never happens, then all doctrine-expressing sentences will be community-specific and incompatibility of the kind envisaged by the NOIA principle will never occur, any more than it does among the grammatical rules of two different natural languages. In addition there is the requirement that there be at least some methods of assessing doctrine-expressing sentences that are not limited in their applicability to just one religious community; if there are no such methods, then apologetics cannot exist as an intellectual discipline.

Third, at least some doctrine-expressing sentences must be capable of truth or falsity. If this turns out not to be the case, then once again incompatibility of the kind envisaged by the principle will not occur, for at least one of the kinds of incompatibility (and perhaps the most interesting) envisaged by that principle, that of a strictly logical kind — such that if doctrine-expressing sentence A is true, doctrine-expressing sentence B must be false — will also never obtain.

There are objections, some of them powerful, to all of these three requirements, and I shall discuss them in the remainder of this chapter,

19

together with examples that should make matters a little clearer. But before I do, I should like to make a broad historical claim that is, I think (although there are doubtless some exceptions), true for the attitudes taken toward their doctrine-expressing sentences by the vast majority of the representative intellectuals of those religious communities belonging to the so-called world religions. I shall then enunciate an interpretive principle based on this historical claim. The claim and the principle will guide the discussion that follows; one of the intended results of employing them, as will become obvious, is to shift the burden of proof.

The historical claim, then, is that most representative intellectuals of most religious communities at most times have thought of themselves, when articulating doctrine-expressing sentences, to be producing artifacts that possess all the three attributes of doctrine-expressing sentences mentioned. That is, representative intellectuals of religious communities have typically tended to think of the sentences they construct as being capable of comprehension outside their own community; as extending their claims beyond the bounds of their own community; and as being, simply, both true and important. Indeed, I constructed the NOIA principle largely with this historical understanding of what the representative intellectuals of religious communities have thought (and, largely, still do think) about what they are engaged in.

It would be tedious, and quite beyond the scope of this study, to support this thesis by enumerating examples. I trust that its truth is sufficiently obvious not to need such demonstration. How else, for example, can one understand the missionary imperative that is such an important part of the thought and action of so many religious communities? It seems clear enough that Buddhists have typically regarded the four noble truths as possessing universal truth, and as being comprehensible to, applicable to, and desirable for non-Buddhists. Similarly for Christians and the salvific significance of Jesus Christ, and for Muslims and the revelatory significance of the Qur'an.

I shall call the interpretive principle to be derived from this historical claim the principle of hermeneutical charity. This, briefly stated, says that, all other things being equal, one should take representative intellectuals of a religious community to be engaged in the kind of intellectual discipline in which they think they are engaged when constructing doctrine-expressing sentences. Doing this at least gives the object of one's study the dignity of being taken seriously as a contributor to the enterprise at which they thought they were working. So if, after detailed historical study, one comes to the mature conclusion (as one must) that people such as Dogen, Augustine, Maimonides, al-Ghazali, and Ramanuja took themselves, by and large, to be engaged in the production of doctrine-expressing sentences with universal applicability because they also took these sentences to be true, it is preferable to consider these representative intellectuals as engaged in just what they thought they were engaged in.

Any other strategy runs the risk of severely distorting the object of one's study, of telling those with whom one is intellectually engaged not that their conclusions are wrong, but that they are not even playing the game they think they are playing. It is one thing to tell an asserter of the doctrine-expressing sentence *all human beings will eventually enter Nirvana* that the sentence is false because there are some human beings who will not enter Nirvana, or because Nirvana is not a condition that anyone can enter; it is quite another to claim that the intellectual who asserts such a sentence is not in fact making universalizable claims about Nirvana and human persons, but instead asserting something that is likely, for specifiable contingent causes, to be credible only to a given community, and that has no purchase, no claim to interest or significance, outside that community.

The historical claim and the interpretive principle stated in the preceding paragraphs are intended mostly to shift the burden of proof. They do not show by themselves (even if the substantive claims they make are true and the recommendations they embody acceptable) that the representative intellectuals of religious communities are correct in their view that their own doctrine-expressing sentences have the properties they take them to have. There might still be pressing theoretical reasons that force the conclusion that one cannot properly consider doctrine-expressing sentences in the same light in which they were considered by their framers. But if there are such reasons, it needs to be shown what they are and arguments need to be offered in their support. The burden of proof is thus shifted to those who would claim that doctrine-expressing sentences must lack one or more of the three key characteristics that the NOIA principle assumes them to possess. To attempts to show this I now turn, considering first those theoretical perspectives that suggest that the doctrine-expressing sentences of one religious community cannot be understood by anyone outside that community.

2.1 THE COMPREHENSIBILITY OF DOCTRINE-EXPRESSING SENTENCES

There is a famous (though no doubt apocryphal) story of a professor of Eastern religions at a prestigious Ivy League university who began all his courses by saying that no one outside the cultures about which he was teaching could possibly hope to understand them. Since he was himself American, as also were most of his students, it eventually became necessary to point out to him that if his thesis were true, it would mean that he was being paid to teach something he did not himself understand to those who could not hope to comprehend it. This is not an encouraging professional position in which to find oneself, and the gentleman in question was forced to at least stop putting the issue so bluntly. The issue raised by the story is, however, an intellectually serious one, and it deserves some discussion.

Are the doctrine-expressing sentences of one religious community comprehensible to anyone who is not a member of that community? An extreme form of the thesis that they are not would run something like this: no representative intellectual from any particular religious community can understand anything at all of the meaning of a doctrine-expressing sentence constructed by the representative intellectuals of another religious community. Let us call this the *mutual incomprehensibility thesis*. From it follows the conclusion that any restatement (or translation) of a doctrine-expressing sentence of one religious community by the representative intellectuals of another is for them as good as any other.

For example: suppose representative intellectuals of a particular Christian community come across a Buddhist doctrine-expressing sentence in the natural language of Sanskrit, which reads: *na bhavo napi cabhavo buddhatvam tena kathyate*. If these Christian intellectuals know some Sanskrit, they might plausibly translate this *therefore Buddhahood is to be described neither as existent nor as nonexistent*. But if, *per impossibile*, such intellectuals were advocates of the mutual incomprehensibility thesis, they would judge the English sentence *baseball is vastly superior to cricket as a spectator sport* to be equally defensible as a representation or translation of the Buddhist doctrine-expressing sentence's meaning. Because that meaning is utterly inaccessible to them and to their community, any translation of it is (for them and their community) as good as any other.

Now, no one (or hardly anyone) holds this lunatic view, not least because it is self-defeating. In order to know that the mutual incomprehensibility thesis is true, one would have to know enough about the doctrine-expressing sentences of some religious community other than one's own to know that one cannot understand them. And yet the mutual incomprehensibility thesis does not allow even this degree of knowledge. It is, nevertheless, important to mention this peculiarly strong form of the mutual incomprehensibility thesis, together with its implications, because it exhibits in a strong degree a feature of many of the intellectual perspectives to be discussed in this and subsequent chapters: that is, the application of an equivalence-principle to all doctrine-expressing sentences.

The principle of equivalence applied here claims that all translational representations of the doctrine-expressing sentences of one religious community by members of some other community are equally good (or equally bad) from the viewpoint of the community doing the translating. Other principles of equivalence, beloved of relativists and antirealists of various stripes, might claim that all doctrine-expressing sentences of all religious communities are equally true, or equally transformative, or equally aesthetically pleasing, or equally credible, or equally whatever you please.

This feature of antirealist reasoning is important because it is designed to call into question an equally important feature of realist perspectives such as that defended in this work. Realist perspectives rest upon the assumption that some forms of discourse are privileged over others; that some doctrine-expressing sentences express true propositions and others do not; that some arguments for the truth of some doctrine-expressing sentences are demonstrative, and others are not. At this point I can do no more than note this fundamental disagreement; I shall return to it at various points in this chapter.

The strong form of the mutual incomprehensibility thesis can, then, safely be left aside. There remain a number of weaker forms of the thesis that are more relevant to our discussion. These grow out of two kinds of worries, both of which have some substance but neither of which is such as to make inevitable the abandonment of the view of doctrine-expressing sentences contained in the NOIA principle. The first worry is about the indeterminacy of meaning (and thus also of translation); the second is a worry about the limits of understanding. I shall consider each in turn.

The objects of our discussion are sentences in natural languages. Collections of these sentences form texts. Sentences, and texts, are composed of signifiers, semantic units, the range of which can be specified only in terms of other signifiers employed by the recipient (the reader or the hearer) of the text. Each signifier has deep and complex roots in a broader semantic field, roots whose nature and extent can never be completely and determinately specified, for they have no determinate extent. They are exhausted neither by what was consciously present to the mind of the fabricator of the text at the moment of fabrication, nor by what is present to the mind of the text's recipient at the time of hearing or reading. As I write this comparatively simple English sentence, the signifiers that constitute it have a semantic range much broader than I know; thus also much broader than I can intend. The same is true for you as you read them. All readers will, in fact, constitute the meaning(s) of the text they receive differently, often significantly or even drastically so. And it will often, given what the disciples of Roland Barthes and Jacques Derrida like to refer to as the "free play of signifiers," be difficult or impossible to distinguish one (re)constitution of a text's meaning from another in terms of rightness or wrongness. Therein lies the glory of reading and writing; if texts did possess a determinate meaning, human boredom would long since have ended their production.

This is one version of a worry about the indeterminacy of meaning. To put matters rather more technically: even in the case of apparently simple signifiers like "rabbit" (and here the work of W.V.O. Quine and his successors can be appropriately joined with that of Jacques Derrida and his), precise specification of extension (the range of things in the nonlinguistic cosmos to which the signifier in question refers) can only be given in dependence upon a wide range of other linguistic bits and pieces that are themselves rooted in a complex and indeterminate semantic field. There is no denaturalized language that fixes extension or precisely determines reference; and in translating the doctrine-expressing sentences of one religious community into the natural-language doctrine-expressing sentences of another, the "correct" translation will always be underdetermined by the available data. To put this another way: there will always be a range of translations apparently equally (though differently) reflective of an understanding of the "meaning" of the original. Every translation flirts with the original; none is married to it. And this applies just as much within the boundaries of natural languages as across them.

All this can be linked with worries about understanding and its limits. We do not have to go to the lengths of our apocryphal professor of Eastern religions to recognize that there are indeed limits placed upon the understanding of the doctrine-expressing sentences of one religious community available to those who are not members of it. This is for a wide variety of reasons. Most generally, the enunciation of a doctrine-expressing sentence by the representative intellectuals of some religious community and its reception by the practising members of that religious community is a far more complex event than the speaking and decoding of sets of signifiers.

The uttering of the sentence *I take refuge in the Buddha* by a devout Buddhist will often come out of and contain a full and rich narrative knowledge of what a Buddha is, a knowledge gained in and through the corpus of literature known as *Jataka*. It may also be embedded in a complex of ritual practices and in a large body of unarticulated beliefs about the nature of the cosmos and the destiny of the human person. And all of this is largely—though not entirely—inaccessible to a non-Buddhist. Similarly, mutatis mutandis, many of the doctrine-expressing sentences uttered by Christians are not going to be understood in all their richness and complexity by those outside the Christian community. The thought-patterns, language-habits, and lifeways produced by acculturation into Christianity by daily use of (say) the *Book of Common Prayer* can be duplicated in no other way than through a lifelong process of acculturation.

But all of this is to say little more than that the understanding of an outsider is not, and can never be, like that of an insider. (The outsider can, of course, become an insider. But that is quite a different matter.) I, as an Englishman, can never know what it is like to have been raised as an American; I, married as I am to my spouse, can never know as you know what it means to be married to yours. These limitations, severe though they are in both extent and kind, do not place anything close to an absolute bar upon understanding, especially if that which the outsider is trying to understand is not so much what it is like to be a member of a religious community other than one's own, but rather the doctrine-expressing sentences produced by that other religious community. Even then, the understanding of the insider and that of the outsider will be different; but the outsider certainly has access to some of what the insider knows, and in certain interesting respects can have access to certain facets of what it is to be an insider, which are not available to the true insider. Understanding, then, like meaning, is not a determinate affair. It is not something that one either has or does not have; rather, it is a matter of degrees and kinds; one can at least approach asymptotically the illusory goal of complete understanding.

Neither of these worries about the indeterminacy of meaning and the unattainability of complete understanding need lead, therefore, to acceptance of any version of the mutual incomprehensibility thesis. The limits and possibilities of understanding, as well as the extent to which the meaning of doctrine-expressing sentences is not determinate, might become clearer with the brief exploration of an example. Suppose outsiders (in this case non-Buddhist and non-Tibetan) who understand written classical Tibetan happen across the Tibetan sentence *yongs su smin pa'i 'og tu thams cad mkhyen pa nyid de* in a text that they know to be authoritative for Gelukpa Buddhists. Their knowledge of the language will enable them to arrive at a lexical translation of the sentence into the home language of their own religious community (which, for the sake of convenience, let us suppose to be English). The translation might be *the condition of omniscience follows upon maturity*. Outsiders might further explore the complex semantic range of the signifiers in this doctrine-expressing sentence in the literature that predates and influences the text in which they found it, looking for glosses, interpretive discussions, and the like. They might then look at how the meaning(s) of the sentence are constituted by the textual and oral tradition that postdates these texts. Especially relevant here would be the consultation of written commentaries and of oral teachings given by contemporary living intellectuals belonging to the tradition. All of this would not enable them to arrive at a single correct interpretation of the sentence, much less to comprehend and communicate a single determinate meaning for it. It would, however, enable them to apprehend (some of) the nuances and complexities of the sentence as its meaning(s) are constituted by the tradition, and (important for our purposes) to rule out certain interpretations as inappropriate.

Outsiders would soon learn to jettison any tendency, should they initially have possessed it, to see in the sentence a veiled esoteric reference to the leg-before-wicket rule in the game of cricket. They would approach more and more closely to an understanding of the sentence in accord with that of the religious community that preserves it and takes it to be expressive of a doctrine. They would still not, of course, apprehend the sentence as would someone acculturated into the tradition; the possibility of attaining omniscience as a Buddha would not, in virtue of their study, become a lived reality for them. But—and this is important—there is no reason to suppose that they might not come to understand more about the truth-conditions and entailments of the doctrine-expressing sentence in question than any living member of the community for whom it is a doctrine-expressing sentence. This probably happens rarely; but there are no theoretical reasons for supposing that it cannot.

One factor that makes this possible is the tendency of members of religious communities not to think in any very self-conscious way about the implications of the views into which they have been acculturated. These views are part of their blood and bone, among the presuppositions of their existence as human beings. They are not typically regarded as matter for logical analysis. That omniscience is an attribute of all Buddhas, and that such omniscience follows directly from the virtuoso religious practices that lead to Buddhahood (this is something of what the term "maturity" means), is accepted and richly understood by the insider. But the ability and the desire to subject the sentence in question to analysis, to draw out its entailments and truth conditions, is likely to be present only in a very few virtuoso intellectual members of any religious community. Outsiders are likely to have more interest in such activities, to engage in them with more persistence, and thus to come to a significantly more subtle and developed understanding of the logical relations among the doctrine-expressing sentences of a community to which they do not belong than is the case for most insiders. The representative intellectuals of religious communities are typically forced into such modes of thought primarily by pressures from outside or by criticisms from dissident groups within: these were the situations in which, for example, Christians felt the need to state their doctrine-expressing sentences in credal formulae. Thus the attempts of an outsider to comprehend the doctrine-expressing sentences of insiders can be valuable for those insiders. This too is a theme to which I shall return.

The considerations offered in the immediately preceding paragraphs are meant to show that there are no pressing theoretical reasons for adopting any version of the mutual incomprehensibility thesis. They are meant also to preserve sensitivity to the nature and extent of the indeterminacy of meaning and to the difficulties inherent in attaining understanding of a complex intellectual phenomenon beyond the bounds of one's own religious community. The NOIA principle thus stands against any version of the mutual incomprehensibility thesis.

It should also be observed, finally, that there are perfectly good indicators as to the adequacy of one's understanding of the doctrine-expressing sentences of a religious community other than one's own, indicators that are usually relatively easy of access. One simply has to go and try out one's understanding of a particular doctrine-expressing sentence on a representative intellectual (or, preferably, more than one) of the religious community for which it is a doctrine-expressing sentence. Being met with such responses as "No, that's all wrong because . . ." should lead to some rethinking. More positive responses are grounds for (cautious) optimism.

I shall return to this set of issues in chapters 5 and 6. At this point, assuming that the doctrine-expressing sentences of different religious communities are (or at least may be) mutually comprehensible, I now need to take up the question of whether, being mutually comprehensible, they might nevertheless be incommensurable.

2.2 THE COMMENSURABILITY OF DOCTRINE-EXPRESSING SENTENCES

The second requirement placed upon doctrine-expressing sentences by the NOIA principle is that at least some of these claims must extend beyond the bounds of the community that gave them birth, and that at least some criteria for the assessment of these claims must also be applicable across these borders. If neither of these things obtains, the result is strict incommensurability: the claim that there are no criteria used for the assessment of doctrine-expressing sentences, for decisions as to which candidates for such status are acceptable and which are not, and as to which doctrine-expressing sentences, once accepted as such, are true and which false, that extend beyond the boundaries of particular communities. Let us call this the *strict incommensurability thesis*.

An adherent of the strict incommensurability thesis typically argues that each doctrine-expressing sentence is given both sense and the possibility of use by the conceptual and cultural context within which it is asserted and believed. Criteria for distinguishing what is sensible and useful from what is neither are, the argument continues, internal to and specific to a given conceptual and cultural context. Like the rules of soccer or the conventions governing the use of prepositions in the English language, they have no purchase and often no sense outside the systems to which they apply. So, to apply the analogy, the criteria that control what can be asserted and believed to be true within the community of Anglican Christians are said to be specific to that community. They cannot be measured or assessed by criteria drawn from outside; to do so is to make the same kind of category mistake that would be made by a soccer player who accused a player of American football of offending, while playing the latter game, against the (soccer) rule forbidding handling of the ball. What is a rule for one game is not a rule for others, and the collection of rules that conjointly constitutes the governing conventions of a particular game uniquely identifies that game over against all others.

I shall return to the idea that doctrine-expressing sentences are significantly like rules, and thus significantly unlike claims about reality, later in this chapter; at this point what interests me is the incommensurability aspect of the thesis. The claim is that there are no criteria of assessment that apply across the boundaries of specific religious communities; that there are no intercommunity methods of argument; and that the construction of community-neutral criteria and methods for assessment and discrimination (every attempt, that is, at apologetics) is impossible because every attempt at constructing such criteria and such methods of argument is necessarily made by someone located within a specific community. There are therefore no reasons but only causes, and all the scholar or the religious believer can do is to try to understand and provide a descriptive account of what functions causally within religious communities other than one's own. They can make no judgements about whether or not people ought to believe what they believe.

One way of understanding the strict incommensurability thesis is to take it as an empirical thesis, a thesis about what is as a matter of fact the case as regards religious communities and their methods of constructing doctrine-expressing sentences and arguing for their truth. Its supporters buttress it, insofar as they can, by appeal to ethnographies that are supposed to reveal religious communities that do in fact have drastically different belief-forming practices and methods of argumentation from each other. Are there then good empirical (or other) reasons for judging the incommensurability thesis to be true? Let us consider an example.

There are religious communities in India whose representative intellectuals look to Ramanuja, a Sanskrit-writing systematic theologian who lived at roughly the same time as Thomas Aquinas, as a figure of definitive authority for their own doctrinal pronouncements. The intellectual tradition that stems from Ramanuja calls itself Vishishtadvaitavedanta, a modified nondualistic form of Vedanta. It is an orthodox (*astika*) school of Hinduism that has been and remains influential upon some aspects of religious thought and practice in India. Briefly (and much too simply) the representative intellectuals of this tradition assert a number of doctrine-expressing sentences (in Sanskrit) that conjointly propound a full-blooded form of theism, according to which the world and the creatures within it are God's body and are enjoined to worship God as their primary duty. Some of the Sanskrit writings produced by the representative intellectuals of this tradition have been translated into English (and into other Western languages); there is no room whatever for doubt that the doctrine-expressing sentences in these documents, and the arguments set forth for their truth, are both comprehensible to (and in some respects identical with) those set forth by the representative intellectuals of Anglican Christianity. No incommensurability here. Disagreement upon some points, certainly; agreement upon others, emphatically; but, throughout, the possibility of understanding and intellectual engagement. The same applies, mutatis mutandis, to the potential on the part of the vishishtadvaita intellectual for understanding and engagement with those English-language writings that have been translated into Sanskrit.

The commensurability adverted to in this case is of course not complete. One criterion for establishing the truth of doctrine-expressing sentences for representative intellectuals of the vishishtadvaita tradition is appeal to a certain body of authoritative texts called *shruti* and *smriti*. This criterion does not travel well; it will clearly not be acceptable to Anglican Christians. So also for Anglican appeals to the sacred texts of the Bible. But a relatively solid and extensive core of commensurability is provided by the fact that certain basic logical principles and argument-forms are regarded as valid (in the former case) and demonstrative (in the latter) by both religious communities. The principles extend at least to the principles of identity, noncontradiction, and excluded middle; the argument forms at least to material implication and contraposition. Thus the representative intellectuals of each religious community are able to recognize and acknowledge a valid argument with true premises offered by those of the other.

Once again, it would be both tedious and beyond the scope of this study to marshal and present the detailed historical evidence that would be required to support this thesis; its truth is, in any event, common knowledge among those historians who have studied the development of logical theory in India and in the West.

Here, then, is one example that serves to counter even the weaker forms of the incommensurability thesis. The adherent of the incommensurability thesis may reply that the example I have chosen is a special (and easy) case. Sanskrit and English, after all, are both Indo-European languages; they share a good deal in terms of vocabulary, linguistic structure, and so forth. And since there is an intimate link between the natural language used by a given religious community and the argument-forms and belief-forming practices used by that community, it is surely not surprising that a good deal of mutual comprehensibility obtains between two religious communities that use natural languages belonging to the same family. Incommensurability, the argument will continue, may still obtain between religious communities whose natural languages belong to quite different families.

And so it may. To show, at least, that there are cases in which it does not, let us consider the possibilities that existed for mutual comprehension between the Arabic-speaking representative intellectuals of some Islamic communities in the medieval period, and their opposite numbers in the Christian communities of Europe during the same period. These latter largely wrote in Latin, and were influenced by what they knew of the Greek intellectual tradition. The Greco-Latin languages are historically not related to the Semitic group, of which Arabic is a member; they share, historically, little in vocabulary and virtually nothing in phonology or syntax. And yet, notoriously, the level of communication and understanding between the representative intellectuals of medieval Islam and those of medieval European Christianity was, if not high, at least very far from nonexistent. The intellectuals of Islam were, for several centuries, the guardians and preservers of much of the Aristotelian corpus (in Arabic versions); later, there were extensive debates back and forth on such complex issues as the doctrine of the incarnation, the nature of the Qur'an as a revelation of God, and so forth. While much that Peter the Venerable, the twelfth-century abbot of Cluny, for example, had to say about Islam was no doubt misguided, there is little reason to suppose that everything was; similarly for al-Ghazali and the Greek intellectual tradition. Again, the common ground in argument forms and logical principles is extensive.

How, then, is an instance of mutual comprehensibility and commensurability between religious communities whose natural languages are not connected to be explained by an adherent of the incommensurability thesis?

It might be argued here that this case also is too easy because of the many historical connections between Islam and Christianity. From some perspectives, after all, Islam is a Christian sect; it was treated as a Christian heresy, not as another religion, by the earliest Christian thinkers to discuss it. And its own view of itself is usually that it is the proper fulfillment of Christianity and Judaism. So, an adherent of the incommensurability thesis might say, it is scarcely surprising that there is a good deal of commensurability between the doctrine-expressing sentences of medieval Islam and those of medieval Christianity. And so it may be. But at this point our incommensurabilists, if I may call them such, begin to sound a little desperate. If the examples of commensurability I have briefly outlined here are defensible, then we have at least two instances of religious communities whose criteria for the assessment of doctrine-expressing sentences extend beyond their own boundaries. They are, moreover, rather significant examples, embracing as they do a goodly number of Hindu, Muslim, and Christian religious communities. It would not be difficult to construct more examples.

I conclude that there are no good reasons to accept the strict incommensurability thesis. While it still may be the case that strict incommensurability obtains among the doctrine-expressing sentences of some religious communities, it begins to seem as though it does not do so among all; and I am in fact not aware of any convincing example of strict (in the sense of "complete") incommensurability between any two religious communities.

Two caveats need to be entered here. First, I am not claiming that commensurability is ever complete, that there are ever examples of simple identity between the criteria used for the assessment of arguments and the discrimination of doctrine-expressing sentences by any two specific religious communities. I have already referred to the incommensurability introduced by appeal to differing sources of (scriptural) authority, and there are many other such cases. More will be said about them in chapters 5 and 6. Commensurability, like understanding and unlike uniqueness, is a matter of degree; fortunately, there appears to be enough of it about to allow the NOIA principle to get off the ground.

Second, commensurability is not the same as agreement. The sets of doctrine-expressing sentences asserted by two different religious communities may very well be in deep and radical disagreement upon all sorts of things even when they are (more or less) commensurable.

The arguments discussed so far suggest that the doctrine-expressing sentences constructed by the representative intellectuals of one religious community are neither always incomprehensible to the representative intellectuals of other religious communities, nor always incommensurable with them. The possibility that such incomprehensibility and such incommensurability may sometimes obtain has been left open; but the burden of proof is upon those who wish to show that it does. The first two conditions upon doctrine-expressing sentences implicit in the NOIA principle (that at least some doctrine-expressing sentences must be capable of being understood outside the community that formed them, and that there must be some criteria for the assessment of such sentences that are not community-specific) thus appear to be met.

I shall now turn to the third: Is it really the case, as it appears on the surface to be, that doctrine-expressing sentences typically make universal claims to truth? That they are bearers of truth and falsity? There are intellectual perspectives that claim that this is a misreading of (most or all) of the doctrine-expressing sentences of religious communities; and to the more important of these I now turn.

2.3 THE COGNITIVE CONTENT OF DOCTRINE-EXPRESSING SENTENCES

The third condition upon doctrine-expressing sentences implicit in the NOIA principle is that they should have cognitive content. That is to say, they should be capable of being true (or false), and so of producing knowledge (when true) in those who assent to them. Further, it should be the case that the knowledge so produced is of a universal kind: it must extend beyond the bounds of the community that produced it. I have already said something about this in my discussion of incommensurability, but further comments will have to be made here.

The NOIA principle suggests that the doctrine-expressing sentences of religious communities typically (though not always) have cognitive content in that they are capable of being true or false, and that this cognitive content extends beyond the bounds of the community that produced them. Let us call this the cognitive realist's view of doctrine-expressing sentences. Given also the principle of hermeneutical charity adverted to above, and the shifting of the burden of proof that goes with it, I shall now explore what I take to be the three most important complexes of views that would deny the cognitive realist's view of (most) doctrine-expressing sentences.

2.3.1 Conceptual Relativism

I have tried to show that one way of denying cognitive realism with respect to doctrine-expressing sentences is to assert some form of incommensurability among the doctrine-expressing sentences of different religious communities. This, as I have suggested, tends to be an empirical thesis about the presence or absence of criteria that extend across the boundaries of religious communities for assessment of and discrimination among doctrine-expressing sentences. I have also argued that there appear to be no good reasons for accepting the stronger versions of the incommensurability thesis, largely because there are many significant counterexamples to it.

Adherents of conceptual relativism, however, go beyond the empiricism of the incommensurability thesis to argue that there are pressing theoretical reasons for believing that even if there are, or at least appear empirically to be, criteria for such assessment and such discrimination that extend across the boundaries of religious communities, the application of these cannot lead to apprehension of the kind of truth desired by the cognitive realist. Let us consider the following version of conceptual relativism; it applies, as this complex of views typically does, a principle of equivalence to all doctrine-expressing sentences:

All doctrine-expressing sentences are equal with respect to the causes of their credibility for those who believe in them; talk of the truth of doctrine-expressing sentences can be reduced, without remainder, to talk of the causes of their credibility for those who believe in them.

This is a principle of equivalence because it says that all doctrine-expressing sentences are equivalent in at least one important respect: they are all equally credible to those (individuals or communities) who believe them. (I shall use "believe" as a convenient shorthand in what follows for "assent to" or "assert as true.") The use of some principle of equivalence or other (that given is perhaps the most common among the more sophisticated versions of conceptual relativism) is an almost universal feature of relativistic views; this is because their basic intellectual goal is to make it impossible to discriminate among doctrine-expressing sentences in regard to truth or falsity; such discrimination is, in contrast, a characteristic desire of the cognitive realist.

The principle of equivalence need not, of course, be that given here. It could be something much less considered, such as the principle of equivalence that all doctrine-expressing sentences are equal with respect to their truth, where "truth" is understood on something like the propositional model already adverted to. But this is a naive principle of equivalence, offered often enough in freshman classrooms, but easy to refute as self-referentially incoherent. The principle of equivalence with respect to causes of credibility is more interesting and more subtle, and therefore also more worthy of time spent in examining it.

This relativistic thesis, then, entails the truth of the proposition that, for all doctrine-expressing sentences and all believers in them, there are causes that make the sentences credible to the believers. This seems unexceptionable. It is probably a universal (though rather uninteresting) truth that no believer in any doctrine-expressing sentence comes to belief causelessly: in every case there will be causes that make them believe it and make it credible to them (two different things). Suppose, for example, I am a Buddhist who assents to the doctrine-expressing sentence *there is, at any given time, an infinite number of Buddhas preaching the dharma in an infinite number of world-realms.* Suppose further that I am a nonintellectual Buddhist, one with no interest in philosophizing and thus no interest in understanding, constructing, or assessing arguments for the truth of the doctrine-expressing sentences to which I assent. In such a case there will, naturally, still be causes that make the sentence in question credible for me. Such causes are likely to include the fact that representative intellectuals of my community authoritatively assert that the sentence is indeed true; that it coheres with and makes sense of certain ritual practices that I frequently undertake, practices that give meaning to my life — and so forth.

Suppose, to take another example, that I am an illiterate Christian in Chicago or Buenos Aires who habitually attends church and recites the Nicene Creed, thus apparently affirming belief in the consubstantiality of God the Father and God the Son. It is likely that the causes of the credibility of the relevant sentences from the creed for me will include: the fact that I learned them catechetically; the fact that they are asserted by the representative intellectuals of my community; the fact that I know lots of stories about Jesus of Nazareth with which these sentences are at least not obviously in contradiction and which they may coherently be taken to illuminate — and so forth.

Some such account, I suspect, could be given for all doctrine-expressing sentences and all believers. But the relativistic thesis under discussion goes much further than this: it claims that all doctrine-expressing sentences are equivalent in the causes of their credibility. That is, there are no doctrine-expressing sentences the causes of whose credibility have any higher status or greater significance than those of any other. To put this another way: a supporter of the relativistic thesis wants to do away with the distinction commonly made between causes and reasons. The former, it would be said by a cognitive realist, comprises the very large set of those causal determinants that influence assent to a doctrine-expressing sentence by any person. This set will include (in addition to the points already canvassed) such things as the peripheral (but essential) fact of being acculturated into a religious community wherein such doctrine-expressing sentences are commonly asserted; being cognizant of the natural language in which they are asserted — and so forth. But these causal determinants, it will be said, are not the same as reasons. Reasons, while forming only a small subset of the much larger set of causes, are what really count because there is a special privileged relationship between them and the truth of the doctrine-expressing sentences to which they relate, a relationship that does not obtain between causes and the doctrine-expressing sentences to which they relate.

So, while it is true that acquaintance with the natural language of Sanskrit might be a necessary condition for assent to the Buddhist doctrine-expressing sentence *shunyah sarvabhavah (all existents are empty)*, and is thus among the causes of its assertibility (and so, by extension, also of its credibility) for those who assert it, such acquaintance contributes nothing to the likelihood of the doctrine-expressing sentence in question being true. The existence, by contrast, of a prima facie demonstrative argument for its truth, and an acquaintance with that argument on the part of a particular believer, does make such a contribution. So runs the argument of the cognitive realist.

This, it would seem, is the heart of the disagreement between the conceptual relativist and the cognitive realist; I have already adverted to it. The former denies that there is any meaningful distinction between reasons and causes; the latter asserts that there is. The former asserts that the job of the scholar in assessing why a particular individual or group assents to a particular set of doctrine-expressing sentences is limited of necessity to a descriptive analysis of the causes (psychological, sociological, economic, and so forth) that make these sentences credible to those who assert them; the latter wants to go further and engage in the normative task of distinguishing between the contingent causes that give a doctrine-expressing sentence credibility for some believer, and the noncontingent reasons for that doctrine-expressing sentence being true. Before discussing how to adjudicate a disagreement as deep as this one, it is worth offering some comments on why, in certain academic circles, various forms of relativism have been so attractive.

Cognitive realism rests, I have already suggested, upon a distinction between privileged and nonprivileged discourse, claims that bear truth and claims that do not, arguments that are demonstrative and arguments that are not. Historically it has been the case that the representative intellectuals of religious communities have assumed that their discourse, their doctrine-expressing sentences, and their arguments are privileged, while those of others are not. When such an assumption is coupled with the economic or military dominance of one cultural group over others, as it was, for example, during the time of European colonial expansion in Asia and Africa, and as it is now in the increasing influence of the USA over the cultures of Latin America, the results can be quite unpleasant. The doctrine-expressing sentences of religious communities in the dominant cultural group can be used as weapons in the service of colonial aggression, economic exploitation, and overt evangelism, and when this happens they come to be seen by members of the religious communities in the economically and militarily subordinate cultures as simple instruments of oppression. Atrocities can then be (and are) committed in the name of the truth of certain doctrine-expressing sentences: one can use (as Christian missionaries often have) the concluding words of the Gospel of Matthew as a basis for the subordination (and even for the abolition) of non-Christian religious communities, just as one can use (as Buddhist intellectual militants in Sri Lanka now often do) the *Dipavamsa* and the *Mahavamsa* as a basis for anti-Tamil violence. These are texts that can be read as providing a religious mandate for the view that Buddhism, and with it the Sinhala language, should dominate the languages and cultures of other (non-Buddhist) groups.

This kind of thing produces a quite proper revulsion among historians, anthropologists, and sociologists; while the revulsion has spread more slowly among theologians, even they have eventually come to feel it, and it is now an integral part of the intellectual equipment of most right-thinking liberal theologians. Suggesting that someone else's revered doctrine-expressing sentence is false thus comes to be seen as an instance of intellectual terrorism only one step removed from the military variety.

When all of this is coupled with the realization, born above all else of anthropological fieldwork and of life in an increasingly pluralistic society, that persons belonging to religious communities other than one's own assert doctrine-expressing sentences with every bit as much sincerity and passion as that used by those in one's own religious community, even when their doctrine-expressing sentences seem exceedingly odd and one's own seem obviously true, the move to some kind of relativistic thesis becomes at least comprehensible and perhaps even natural. If one renounces the idea of a privileged discourse, the idea that some arguments are good and some bad, that some doctrine-expressing sentences are true and some false, and replaces it with the fundamental relativistic intuition that all arguments and all doctrine-expressing sentences are in some sense on a par, one will then also have renounced cultural and intellectual imperialism with all their attendant evils.

The intuition is stubborn, though, that a proper distinction can be made between reasons and causes, and that some kinds of discourse actually are privileged. It is especially stubborn among the representative intellectuals of religious communities for the very good reason that, as I have already suggested, the doctrine-expressing sentences formulated by such people tend to make ultimate claims — claims about the way things really are, about the way people should really live, and about the origin and destiny of all things. Such ultimate claims do not sit very easily with the relativistic thesis stated above: the claims in question would lose their power and their interest if they were taken by those who construct them (as they typically are not) to express the contingent fact of credibility rather than the noncontingent one of truth.

Can the intuition that there is a proper distinction to be made between reasons and causes be further supported? I have suggested that this intuition appears to have been shared by the vast majority of the representative intellectuals of religious communities throughout human history, and that pursuing it has the major conceptual and interpretive advantage of adequately representing doctrine-expressing sentences as they were (and are) understood by their promulgators. But relativists typically demand more than this: they demand a demonstrative argument for the truth of the thesis that there is some privileged discourse, as well as a delineation of its extent and limits.

Such a demand cannot, I think, be met by the cognitive realist. It is notoriously difficult, for example, to give a demonstration of the validity of the principle of material implication (*if p then necessarily q; p; therefore q*) which does not already presuppose that principle's validity. I shall make no such attempt here. However, it is far from clear that conceptual relativists are justified in making such a demand. To be consistent, they should simply say that cognitive realism is on a par in the causes of its credibility (for cognitive realists) with relativism (for relativists).

Therefore, in taking a cognitive realist's view of doctrine-expressing sentences in this study I do not feel unduly disconcerted by the lack of a conclusive demonstration of cognitive realism's truth. Precisely the same lack obtains in the case of relativism, and since the principle of hermeneutical charity, together with the historical claim upon which it is based, shifts the burden of proof from realism to relativism, there seems little reason to be perturbed by the relativistic challenge.

A final comment: the most powerful argument offered against cognitive realism by the relativist (at least in the sphere of analyzing doctrine-expressing sentences) is that cognitive realism issues in an unacceptable level of intellectual imperialism, and that it is unacceptably damaging to peace, amity, and concord. There is a good deal of truth in this pragmatic argument, and I shall return to it in chapter 5 when I set forth the conditions under which apologetics may properly be engaged in. But it is important to mention here a counterargument, also pragmatic, which is at least as strong: engagement in apologetics based upon a cognitively realist view of doctrine-expressing sentences is a learning tool of unparalleled power. It makes possible a level of understanding of one's own doctrine-expressing sentences and their logic, as well as those of others, which is not to be had in any other way. This will be further argued in subsequent chapters, and illustrated in the final chapter. It is also important to stress that there is no necessary connection between believing that someone is wrong and acting oppressively, or with aggression, toward them. And to this too I shall return later.

2.3.2 Experiential Expressivism

A second though considerably less radical way in which the cognitive realist's view of doctrine-expressing sentences can be challenged is that enshrined in a complex of views that I shall call experiential expressivism. The experiential expressivist claims, in brief, that all doctrine-expressing sentences are expressive or descriptive of a single, unique, transculturally and translinguistically available religious experience. This view calls into question the cognitive content of most doctrine-expressing sentences because it reduces them to reports of the occurrence and (presumably) the nature of certain experiences. It makes them of the same logical kind as *I see a tree now*; while this is certainly a descriptive report of a certain individual's being appeared to tree-ly at a certain time, and while the appearance witnessed by the utterance of the relevant sentence may be excellent, even conclusive evidence for the (nonexperiential) claim *there is a tree here now*, the former sentence is not primarily about what there is in the world or about the value of such, and thus does not have specifiable cognitive content in the sense required by the NOIA principle. The above analysis can, of course, be applied, mutatis mutandis, to sentences such as the prophet Isaiah's claim to have seen the "Lord seated on a throne, high and exalted" (Isaiah 6:1) in the year of King Uzziah's death, or the claim that one is having a vision of Maitreya, the future Buddha, at the moment.

If the thesis that all doctrine-expressing sentences are descriptive of or expressive of experiences should turn out to be defensible, then it would seem to follow that at least one of the requirements placed upon doctrine-expressing sentences by the NOIA principle cannot be upheld. There are, however, at least two reasons for thinking that experiential expressivism cannot be true.

First, experiential expressivism rests upon a naive view of the relations between experience and discourse. For the experiential expressivist, the relation between religious experience and the construction of doctrine-expressing sentences is one-way: the former produces the latter, and the function of the latter is simply to express the core attributes of the former. This view flies in the face of all that we know from historical, anthropological, and psychological studies about the complex phenomenon of becoming and remaining a member of a religious community. These studies show, I think decisively, that there is an exceedingly complex symbiotic and reciprocal relationship between experience and doctrine; each conditions the other, but if there is a dominant direction of influence it is from doctrine to experience, not vice versa. Assent to a given set of doctrine-expressing sentences (together, of course, with the legends, myths, rituals, practices, and so forth, that accompany it) makes possible the occurrence of certain kinds of experience, and may at times act as both necessary and sufficient condition for the occurrence of that experience.

For the experiential expressivist, experience is the primary determinant, and is usually thought of as somehow prior to and independent of the shaping forces of language and culture. Pure, transcendent, prelinguistic, and preconceptual experience, on this view, gets filtered, funneled, and channeled into the rigid forms controlled by the doctrine-expressing sentences of religious communities. Adherents of such a view also tend to think that this pure transcendent experience lies at the heart of all religious traditions, and that the apparent contradictions and clashes among the doctrine-expressing sentences of religious communities are to be explained by the fact that they formulate and describe this core experience differently, not by any genuine and important disagreement about what is the case. This position will be explored in more detail in chapter 3, under the label "esotericist perspectivalism." At this point in the investigation, I am interested only in the thesis that experience is always prior to and independent of the doctrine-expressing sentences that later come to express it.

Experience is made possible for small children by the development of motor and conceptual skills that act as necessary conditions for its occurrence. A newborn has no sense of the boundary between its own body and the rest of the world; a six-month-old has no sense of other persons as independent centers of identity. The development of these kinds of knowledge is made possible by a combination of increasing physical skills and progressive socialization. The same is true, on the whole, for religious experience. In almost all cases the very possibility of its occurrence depends upon a long-term process of socialization. One learns, for example, the *Jataka* stories as a child and through them internalizes the value of sacrificial compassion and the importance of nonattachment. Later, perhaps, one studies and internalizes key Buddhist doctrine-expressing sentences (this process, in Christian circles, used to be called catechesis) making them real for oneself by the process of meditational cultivation (*bhavana*). And so eventually one becomes "Buddhist," assenting to a certain set of doctrine-expressing sentences and using them to shape one's experience.

The symbiotic relations between doctrine and experience cannot easily be broken; and the romantic, quasi-Byronic, thesis that religious experience somehow bursts upon a receptive individual unformed by doctrine and the long process of acculturation into a religious community is nothing more than a romantic fantasy.

There is a second reason for judging experiential expressivism to be false. Even leaving aside the criticisms made in the immediately preceding paragraphs, it is implausible to claim that all doctrine-expressing sentences are expressive of experience in any direct way. Those sentences for which such a claim is most immediately plausible are direct first-person reports, such as the words quoted earlier from the book of the prophet Isaiah. But such reports are not, typically, doctrine-expressing sentences (though they sometimes may be). In order to become such, they need to go through a process of abstraction until one arrives at something like *there exists a God who commissions prophets*. Such a doctrine-expressing sentence, while not completely unrelated to experience, is not simply produced by it; and it makes a claim about reality that is true (if it is) independently of whether the representative intellectuals of the religious community that asserts it as a doctrine-expressing sentence have ever had the experience of being commissioned as a prophet. Then, of course, there are doctrine-expressing sentences whose relationship to experience is still more tenuous. Consider:

The Nicene Creed, and that which is commonly called the Apostles' Creed, ought thoroughly to be received and believed: for they may be proved by most certain warrants of Holy Scripture.

This is the eighth of the thirty-nine Articles of Religion promulgated as doctrine-expressing sentences by the Anglican Church. It is a doctrine-expressing sentence whose referent is authoritative texts (the creeds mentioned); it prescribes the proper attitude of the community to these texts, and does so by appealing to another set of authoritative texts—Holy Scripture—as warrant. It is difficult to imagine what kind of religious experience this particular doctrine-expressing sentence might express; it is certainly directly expressive of none, and is yet nonetheless clearly a doctrine-expressing sentence of a particular religious community, and, moreover, one that expresses a proposition and so may be true or false.

I conclude that there are no good reasons for accepting the strong varieties of experiential expressivism, and many for thinking that they are false. This mode of calling the cognitive content of the doctrine-expressing sentences of religious communities into question therefore need not be given the kind of credence it would need in order that the NOIA principle should be made inoperative by it.

2.3.3 Rule Theory

It is widely thought by systematic and philosophical theologians today that the doctrine-expressing sentences of religious communities are not and cannot be first-order cognitive claims of the kinds distinguished in this study, but that they are rules, second-order regulative principles governing the life of the community that asserts them. If this thesis is correct, then doctrine-expressing sentences will not have the cognitive content that the NOIA principle requires them to have. They will, moreover, not extend their purchase beyond the bounds of the community whose life they are to govern. How, then, do the arguments run here?

A rule theorist typically wants to develop a model of what religious doctrines are drawn from the work of cultural anthropologists and linguistic theorists. Negatively, they are concerned to reject two other important models: the cognitive realist's model and the experiential expressivist's model. The former, as I have shown, understands doctrine-expressing sentences primarily as expressive of propositions, and so bearers of truth-value and conveyors of information about extramental and extralinguistic realities, while the latter sees them as expressions, descriptions, or symbolic representations of inner experiential states or existential attitudes. In rejecting the cognitive realist's model of doctrine-expressing sentences, the rule theorist seems to call the NOIA principle into question: for if doctrine-expressing sentences cannot make direct claims to truth but can function only regulatively within the bounds of specific communities, then they cannot be directly incompatible. The rule theorist also typically develops a particular view of what it is for a doctrine-expressing sentence to be true, a view that differs significantly from that held by the cognitive realist.

On the cognitive realist's view, to say of a doctrine-expressing sentence that it is true is to say that the proposition expressed by it corresponds to reality. So, for example, when a Buddhist says *everything that exists is momentary*, the proposition thus expressed is true if and only if everything that exists is momentary. For the rule theorist, in contrast, truth is a property not of propositions but of the categories of systems: a religious conceptual system is true if and only if the categories that constitute it make reference to ultimate reality (or some such periphrasis) a possibility. That is, if by using these categories one can talk about whatever the object of religious discourse is taken to be, then the system by which they are constituted is categorially true. On this view, it would seem, one would have to interpret the Buddhist assertion just mentioned as a categorial assertion, an assertion that a given category (and only that category) should be employed in order to make meaningful reference to religious reality possible. It should be understood, that is, as a rule whose content can be paraphrased, roughly, as *it is incumbent upon the Buddhist religious community to use the category of momentariness in talking about reality.*

Now, this view, which sees doctrine-expressing sentences as something like idioms, as cultural-linguistic systems that generate categories and provide rules for which category is to be used when, does not make it impossible that some doctrine-expressing sentences may also make claims to the kind of truth envisaged by the cognitive realist, and may thus oppose one another, as the NOIA principle suggests. More broadly, the rule theorist's position is both defensible and illuminating if all it claims is that some (perhaps even many) doctrine-expressing sentences function for (some) religious communities primarily as rules. But further arguments are needed if the stronger thesis that all doctrine-expressing sentences function only regulatively for all religious communities is to hold.

How might this be done? The rule theorist typically begins by making a distinction between intrasystematic truth and ontological truth. The former is the truth that given utterances have in virtue of their coherence with the total conceptual context in which they occur. A religious utterance would thus be intrasystematically true if and only if it cohered with all other utterances, attitudes, and practices in the religious form of life within which it occured. By contrast, an utterance would be ontologically true if and only if it corresponded to extracategorial reality. A strong version of rule theory would then go on to claim that, for any given religious utterance, intrasystematic truth is a necessary condition for ontological truth.

Imagine a crusader uttering the sentence *christus est dominus* while lopping off the head of an infidel: it would seem that the intrasystematic incoherence of the action with the verbal expression of a discipleship that requires sacrificial peacemaking as an essential component makes the utterance intrasystematically (and so also, on the rule theorist's view, ontologically) false. Or imagine a Buddhist taking the ten precepts while seducing his friend's wife. Since the precepts include a vow to abstain from sexual activity of all kinds, in this case also there is an intrasystematic incoherence between the utterances involved in taking the precepts and the actions involved in the seduction. Conversely, the utterances in question might be true if spoken in a situation wherein they cohere with the total context.

Such an elevation of intrasystematic truth to the status of a necessary condition for ontological truth is, on the face of it, odd. Certainly, if applied to other forms of discourse it leads to manifest absurdities. Suppose, for example, I have a simple conceptual system comprising two propositions: *all seven-year-olds turn green on Thursdays* and *my seven-year-old daughter does not turn green on Thursdays*. Since both propositions are intrasystematically false, it would seem to follow that, according to the rule theorist's view, both must also be ontologically false. And this is manifestly not the case, since the former is false and the latter true. It would seem preferable to say, to return the discussion to doctrine-expressing sentences, not that intrasystematically false religious utterances are false, but that they fail as religious utterances. Their intrasystematic falsity, of pressing concern though it should be to those who have their religious being within the system in question, is effectively neutral in regard to their ontological truth.

I suspect, however, that the rule theorist's reasons for making this apparently implausible claim about the logical relations between intrasystematic and ontological truth have to do with the view that a religious utterance can have ontological truth (that is, a correspondence between what is expressed in the utterance and reality) only when it is a performance, an act or deed that by and through its performance helps create that correspondence. That is, the rule theorist typically wants to say that sentences forming part of religious conceptual systems, doctrine-expressing sentences, can possess ontological truth only when uttered in an appropriately faith-centered confessional setting. This, the argument goes, is because only in such settings can religious utterances gain sufficient referential specificity to be capable of expressing propositions and thus of possessing ontological truth.

A corollary of this view is the position that confessional language is first-order discourse, while the language of technical theology is second-order discourse. The former (and only the former) is capable of expressing propositions, while the latter provides and organizes the categories (the grammar and syntax) that govern which assertions may be made. Church doctrine (technical theology) thus becomes entirely regulative in function, while ontological claims to truth are made only in and through confessional utterance.

It seems worth pursuing some of the implications of this view. To restate the position formally: a religious utterance becomes a true first-order proposition for the rule theorist if and only if all the following four conditions are met: first, that the utterance in question is spoken in a context wherein it is intrasystematically true; second, that the utterance in question is part of a conceptual system that is categorially true; third, that the utterance in question is given voice to in an appropriate confessional context; and fourth, that reality is as the utterance in question says it is. All of these conditions except the third can be met by the doctrine-expressing sentences found in technical theological texts. Why then is this third condition so necessary?

Two reasons are typically offered, and I can think of no others. Neither will do the work the rule theorist needs it to do. First, it is said (or, more often, implied) that a necessary condition for the possession of ontological truth by any given religious utterance is that the utterance in question be performative. By this is meant that a religious utterance must, in order to be ontologically truthful, create a new reality. Suppose the Nicene Creed is recited by a believer in an appropriate liturgical setting: this act may certainly be regarded as an instance of uttering performatively in just this sense. It may be understood as constituting a new relationship between two previously existing relata: the worshiper and God. In this it fits the structure of other more homely examples of performative discourse: apologies, which by their utterance heal a broken relationship; marriage vows, which by their utterance create a union; and so forth. But it cannot be understood as constituting or bringing into existence either of the two relata to which its utterance relates. God exists (if God does) before the utterance, with all of God's essential properties (if God has any), just as God does after the utterance. So does the worshiper. What is changed (newly constituted) is the relation between them. But if this is all that is meant by categorizing religious utterance as performative, not enough has been said to support the rule theorist's third requirement for the possession of ontological truth by a religious utterance — that such an utterance be given voice to in an appropriate confessional context. This is so because among the conditions for the efficacy of every performative religious utterance is the truth of some more or less specifiable nonperformative doctrine-expressing sentences. In the case under consideration these would include *there is a God who made heaven and earth* and *there is an utterer of religious utterances other than God* — and so forth.

To generalize: in order for any performative utterance (religious or otherwise) to function as such, what is expressed by some set of nonperformative utterances must be ontologically true. To suggest, as the rule theorist typically does, that only sentences uttered confessionally and with performative function can possess ontological truth is thus confused. The very use of the category of performative utterance suggests, in fact, not that confessional utterance possesses ontological truth because of its performativity, but rather that ontological truth is never a property of performative utterance, and, because of this, never a property of performative confessional utterance. None of this, of course, is to say that performative utterance is uninteresting or religiously insignificant; only that it cannot, by its very nature, possess ontological truth in the rule theorist's sense.

There is another reason, or set of reasons, offered for the necessity of the rule theorist's third condition for a given religious utterance to possess ontological truth. This is that only by fully entering into the form of life that constitutes a particular religious community can one understand the doctrine-expressing sentences of that community with sufficient richness and precision to be able to utter them with enough referential specificity to give them the possibility of possessing ontological truth. Further, the key terms of the doctrine-expressing sentences in question are given their content largely in and through the use of narratives. How can one know Buddha without knowing the *Jataka* stories? How can one know God without knowing the narratives of the Bible? Theologizing, the rule theorist typically claims, must thus be done "intratextually," in the sense that what normatively constrains it is an agreed text. Briefly, and somewhat crudely, members of religious communities need their stories in order to tell them to whom (or to what) their religious utterances refer.

It is hard to disagree with this. But it is equally hard to see that it is terribly significant. That exposure to and faith in certain stories is a necessary condition for understanding (and even for properly making) religious utterances is surely an important psychological truth for most members of most religious communities; but it is equally obviously not a logical truth. If it were the latter, then a member of a Christian community could neither fully understand nor properly assert (or deny) any Buddhist doctrine-expressing sentences, and vice versa. And the result would be both relativism and fideism: religious communities would become closed, impermeable, incommensurable forms of life.

It should be stressed in conclusion that, even if rule theorists are correct in all their contentions about the practical importance of narrative, intratextuality, and catechesis for both the enterprise of fully understanding religious utterances and the enterprise of creating new members of religious communities (and there are very valuable insights to be found here), no arguments are offered for their logical necessity. There is nothing in the exposition of rule theory given here that suggests that a specific doctrine-expressing sentence cannot possess ontological truth (or be fully comprehended) outside the (almost) closed, intratextually constituted, circle of a particular religious form of life. Much of it suggests that such sentences are very often not fully understood outside the circle, and this is almost certainly correct; but that is a very different matter from claiming that they cannot be.

Finally, the rule theorist's rejection of experiential expressivism is entirely justified. The use of cultural-linguistic models of religion always implicit and sometimes explicit in a rule theoretical approach is also very fruitful, both for our understanding of how religious doctrine (often) functions in communities and in the life of the believer, and for our understanding of how one becomes and remains a member of a religious community. But the rule theorist's espousal of cultural-linguistic models does not require (or even suggest) that only confessional religious utterances can be ontologically true, or that all doctrinal formulations are regulative. The doctrine-expressing sentences of an averagely sophisticated religious community can still (and should still) be seen as capable of bearing truth, and this in no way hinders their ability to function as rules. Taking this view also leaves open the possibility of interesting empirical enquiries into the question of how specific doctrine-expressing sentences do in fact function for specific religious communities.

I suspect, against the rule theorist, that there is no useful a priori answer to this question. It is likely that some doctrine-expressing sentences function both regulatively and propositionally for some religious communities, some only regulatively, and some only propositionally. Those parts, then, of rule theory that can be defended do not require the rejection of interreligious apologetics, positive or negative. The NOIA principle thus stands against these criticisms.

3

Incompatibility among Doctrine-Expressing Sentences

If the NOIA principle is ever to come into operation, it must be the case not only that there is a theoretical possibility of incompatibility among some doctrine-expressing sentences of some religious communities, but also that such incompatibility is sometimes thought to occur by the representative intellectuals of some religious community. It may, of course, also sometimes actually occur; but I am not directly concerned with that question here. If the judgement that there is such incompatibility is never made, the NOIA principle would simply be a conditional whose antecedent is never affirmed; recall that the principle says that *if* representative intellectuals belonging to some specific religious community come to judge at a particular time that some or all of their own doctrine-expressing sentences are incompatible with some alien religious claim(s), *then* they should feel obliged to engage in both positive and negative apologetics vis-à-vis these alien religious claim(s) and their promulgators. In order that the principle should come into operation, the antecedent of this conditional needs occasionally to obtain. Otherwise, the NOIA principle might be of some theoretical interest, but could scarcely have any practical application.

There are a number of perspectives, some currently with great influence among theologians interested in interreligious dialogue, from which it is judged that such incompatibility never obtains. This position may be taken even by those who are prepared to allow theoretically that such incompatibility might occur. Such theorists usually see religious pluralism, the existence of multiple and prima facie incompatible sets of doctrine-expressing sentences, as not only a fact but also a positive value. That is, they tend to regard the apparent incompatibilities among the doctrine-expressing sentences of religious communities as, first, only apparent; and, second, as valuably representing different perspectives upon or reactions to "ultimate reality" or some such abstract periphrasis for the full-blooded religious realities about which the representative intellectuals of religious communities have typically taken themselves to be talking. I shall consider these perspectives under the general label of "perspectivalism," and shall, for heuristic purposes, divide them into two subtypes: universalist perspectivalism and esotericist perspectivalism.

3.1 UNIVERSALIST PERSPECTIVALISM

The *Rigveda*, India's oldest collection of sacred texts, contains the famous line: "Reality is one, though wise men speak of it variously." As it stands, this line is splendidly ambiguous. It may mean that what really exists is of a single nature, and that the fact of its being labeled and analyzed in a variety of ways by those who appear to be wise shows only that they are not as wise as they seem. Or it may mean that everything said by the wise about this single reality is equally true simply in virtue of the fact that it is said by the wise and refers to a single reality. Or ... but the interpretive possibilities are endless.

This gnomic saying has typically been taken as a charter by adherents of universalist perspectivalism, and has been seen as expressing the transcendental truth that, in some sense, the utterances of all religious virtuosi are equally true, or equally transformative, or some such. One often finds this line from the *Rigveda* cited with approval by universalist perspectivalists of many stripes. It is often buttressed by the parable of the blind men and the elephant: four blind men are wandering through the forest one day when they meet an elephant. Each grasps one part of the elephant's body in an attempt to find out what kind of beast this is, and after the animal has passed by they compare notes. One says that the elephant is like a thick and sinuous snake (he has grasped its trunk); another says that it is like a massive and immovable pillar (he has grasped one of its legs); a third says that it is like a high smooth wall whose top he could not reach (he has touched its side); and a fourth says that it is like a smooth, cool, curved piece of rock (he has grasped its tusk). After discussing the matter, the blind men conclude that they must have been touching different beasts, for they can arrive at no single picture that will make sense of their different experiences.

The moral of the story should be clear: there is a single picture that will make sense of all these different experiences, but it is a picture available only to the sighted, not to the blind. So also, it is claimed by our perspectivalists, for religious reality and the claims made about it by the representative intellectuals of religious communities: there is a single religious reality, and also some vantage point for perceiving it, from which apparently incompatible doctrine-expressing sentences can be seen not to be incompatible. The esotericist and elitist overtones of this position will be drawn out when I come to discuss the esotericist variety of perspectivalism. Here I can only note that the story seems to suggest — and is so taken by esotericists — that there is a body of religious virtuosi (the sighted) to whom the proper vantage-point (i.e., that from which the apparent contradictions among doctrine-expressing sentences are resolved) is available, while ordinary religious men and women have no access to such a perspective.

Other images, found in the mystical writings of all or almost all religious communities, are also beloved by perspectivalists: the many roads up a single mountain, using different routes to reach an identical goal; the different rivers emptying themselves into a single ocean in which their waters merge and their differences are abolished—and so forth. While these images are, as they stand, imprecise, they are often used as at least incidental support for claims of this kind:

> The great world faiths embody different perceptions and conceptions of, and correspondingly different responses to, the real or ultimate from within the major variant cultural ways of being human . . . within each of them the transformation of human existence from self-centeredness to Reality-centeredness is manifestly taking place . . . the great religions are to be regarded as alternative soteriological paths within which, or ways along which, men and women can find salvation/liberation/fulfillment.

Almost all the major themes of what I am calling universalist perspectivalism are evident here. The position is perspectivalist in that it claims that religious communities "embody different perceptions and conceptions of, and correspondingly different responses to, the real or ultimate"; it is universalist in that the attempt to discriminate among these different conceptions, to judge that some are adequate and some are not, is rejected. All such conceptions (or at least all those belonging to the "world religions"; there is an equivocation here that as I shall try to show, makes strictly universalist perspectivalism rather hard to defend), it is claimed, transform human existence in desirable ways. They are thus "alternative soteriological paths" that lead to the same goal, and are equally effective in bringing about the desired transformation.

Notice that universalist perspectivalism, like conceptual relativism, applies an equivalence principle to all doctrine-expressing sentences. The view requires that there actually is a single religiously ultimate reality, and that it is of a kind capable of being effectively mediated through a wide variety of incompatible doctrine-expressing sentences. It means, to take an example from Buddhism and Christianity, that ultimate reality must be such that it can be characterized *both* as a set of evanescent instantaneous events connected to one another by specifiable causes but without any substantial independent existence, *and* as an eternal changeless divine personal substance. While it may not be impossible to construct some picture of ultimate reality that meets these demands, it is far from easy to see how it might be done.

It should also be evident that universalist perspectivalism is an a priori position, a position, that is, constructed without much interest in the empirical details of what religious communities actually tend to assert, value, and practice. This is evident from the fact that no empirical evidence as to the extent of incompatibilities among doctrine-expressing sentences is usually allowed to count against its truth.

What one usually finds in the writings of those who adhere to universalist perspectivalism on the question of how it is that the same ultimate reality can be characterized in apparently contradictory ways is a bow in the direction of ineffability: since the ultimate reality transcends all our characterizations of it, we have to make a fundamental distinction between it as it is *an sich* and it as it is apprehended by us. While it may indeed be the case that ultimate reality is, in and of itself, just the kind of thing that can be characterized and mediated in the ways suggested above, the prior probability of this being true seems distressingly low; some powerful collateral reasons to support it are needed.

Some collateral reasons are typically offered. First, one finds an ex post facto justification of the possibility of the truth of universalist perspectivalism, a justification that assumes that it is true. This usually has the following form: if there really is a single transcendent reality, one would expect human characterizations and descriptions of it to differ, perhaps even, allowing for the radical effects of contingent social and cultural factors upon such conceptualization and description, to differ drastically. So the fact that we do find such drastically differing descriptions of the putative ultimate reality is not troubling.

Then there are a couple of reasons usually given for the desirability of adhering to universalist perspectivalism. The first of these has to do with world harmony: if everyone becomes convinced of the truth of this position, then missionaries will pack their bags, Jews, Muslims, and Christians will stop fighting one another in the Middle East, Buddhists and Hindus will stop fighting one another in Sri Lanka, and the world will become a much happier and more habitable place. There is also the suggestion that the sincere and committed believer of any particular religious community often meets sincere and convinced believers of other communities in whom "the fruits of openness to the divine Reality are gloriously apparent."

None of these collateral reasons is able to do the work it needs to do. While it is probably true that much of the violence and bloodshed in the world has something to do with religious hatred, broadly understood, this is not by itself a sufficient reason to deny that instances of such disagreement are cognitively significant. And the recognition that there are good, sincere, and apparently grace-filled individuals in all religious communities does not in any way require that there are no substantive cognitive conflicts among the truth claims of those communities.

There are other, and perhaps more severe, problems with universalist perspectivalism as I have defined it. I shall note only two. First, there is the problem of criteria for exclusion. The thrust of the position is to remove the need for excluding as false or inadequate any doctrine-expressing sentence of significance to any community. And yet this leads rather rapidly to very undesirable conclusions. Consider, for example, the case of the Jonestown massacre: the reverend Jim Jones built up a devoted following in California in the 1970s, and then led the faithful off to await the coming of the kingdom in Guiana. While there the community appears to have degenerated into paranoia and fear, and ended with the founder instructing his followers to drink cyanide. Some complied willingly; others were forced. The end result was the agonizing death of hundreds. What do perspectivalists say about such a case? They would presumably want to exclude a sentence of the form *God is such that God wants God's followers to drink cyanide now* as being properly descriptive of the ultimate reality. Presumably, also, this sentence is not to be regarded as on a par with *God was in Christ reconciling the world to himself* as a means of mediating the ultimate reality to human beings and transforming the quality of their lives. And yet in order to make such nice distinctions, perspectivalists must construct criteria for separating appropriate affirmations about the ultimate reality from inappropriate ones. They must, in other words, enter into apologetical discourse whether they like it or not.

Universalist perspectivalists do tend to acknowledge this problem if pressed. But their suggestions as to criteria by which appropriate affirmations may be distinguished from inappropriate ones are usually thin. Some religious communities, apparently, constitute an effective context for the salvific transformation of their adherents, while others do not. But we are never told how to distinguish the former from the latter, nor what arguments may be brought to bear in support of the distinctions we must make. This lack of interest in such an important matter comes directly from the inner logic of the position: universalist perspectivalism was constructed in an attempt to get away from the need to make such invidious distinctions. To attempt a rational justification of the distinctions that even a perspectivalist must make would be to reenter the apologetical arena, and since doing this is abhorrent, the distinctions are made (as they must be) but not argued for.

In brief: perspectivalists cannot apply an equivalence principle to all doctrine-expressing sentences (e.g., the equivalence principle that all, if assented to, are equally productive of desirable effects), or to all religious communities (e.g., that all are equally effective contexts for the salvific transformation of their members). If they attempt to do so, they end with the extremely undesirable conclusion that members of quasireligious communities such as the SS, or those followers of Jim Jones who died at Jonestown, are being salvifically transformed by their membership to just the same extent as are devout Sunni Muslims or Hasidic Jews. And once this absurdity is rejected, perspectivalists can no longer be properly called "universalist." They, like an ordinary apologist, must elucidate and defend the criteria they use to distinguish between religious communities that are appropriate contexts for salvific transformation and those that are not, between doctrine-expressing sentences whose effects are desirable and those whose effects are not.

The difficulties with universalist perspectivalism may, perhaps, be seen more clearly by taking a particular example of a criterion put forward by adherents of this view to do the essential work of distinguishing between religious communities that are appropriate contexts for salvific transformation and those that are not. Suppose we say that the former espouse doctrines and practices that are observably productive of a transformation in their members from ego-centeredness to reality-centeredness, while the latter espouse doctrines and practices that observably produce no such transformation. And suppose that this is a formal criterion: that is, suppose its key terms, "reality-centeredness" and "ego-centeredness" are given no content. If it is a formal criterion then it cannot do the work it is intended to do; for, observably, a sincere and devoted member of the SS or of the Jonestown community is often capable of actions that appear, dramatically, not to be ego-centered—even to the point of self-sacrificial death. What distinguishes the self-sacrificial death of a stormtrooper in the service of the thousand-year Reich from that of a Christian martyr on the cross? Clearly, not the degree to which the egocentricity of each has been transformed into reality-centeredness; rather, it is the radical difference in the way in which reality is conceived by each.

Suppose, then, that the criterion suggested is a substantive one, in which the key terms are given content. If this route is followed the apologetical enterprise cannot be avoided, for the adherent of universalist perspectivalism is then committed to holding a particular view of reality and to rejecting those that do not comport well with it. Other criteria employed by adherents of universalist perspectivalism are of the same kind and meet the same fate.

There are other more strictly logical problems produced by this tension in the universalist perspectivalist's views. The perspectivalist's position would seem to entail, if taken seriously, that any religious community that claims cognitive superiority for its set of doctrine-expressing sentences over that of another religious tradition must be making a false claim. Yet to assert this is precisely to claim that some of the doctrine-expressing sentences of some religious communities are false, since some communities make just such a claim; and such an interesting and potentially religiously divisive assertion cries out for justification through argument, justification that perspectivalists of a universalist stamp seem not to want to provide.

Universalist perspectivalism would, if true, seriously threaten the NOIA principle. It would make significant clash among the doctrine-expressing sentences of different religious communities effectively impossible, and would thus make the apologetical response (positive or negative) completely inappropriate. But, as I have tried to show, the position is, prima facie, massively implausible, and the collateral arguments offered for its truth do not go far enough toward remedying this implausibility. The NOIA principle thus stands against this set of criticisms.

3.2 ESOTERICIST PERSPECTIVALISM

Esotericist perspectivalism comprises a range of intellectual positions. What they share is a stress on the importance of religious elites, or religious virtuosi, and the esoteric or hidden traditions that are preserved and passed on by such people. Esotericist perspectivalism, of whatever particular stripe, generally puts forward two theoretically separable positions. The first is, on its face, empirical. It consists in the claim that *every religious community contains within it a small group of virtuosi, and the experiences and teachings of these elites are always the same.* The second is normative: it consists in the claim that *the experiences of these virtuoso groups are veridical, and the sentences in which they express their doctrines are true.*

I shall consider the strengths and weaknesses of these positions in turn. But before doing so, a general comment on what is perhaps the strongest aspect of esotericist perspectivalism needs to be made. Esotericist perspectivalists recognize, quite rightly, that the traditional divisions of religious communities and their beliefs into what I have called the polyglot semifictional multicultural entities of Buddhism, Christianity, and the like, are very often not the best way of considering the issues that cluster around the fact of religious pluralism. They recognize that doctrinal agreements and disagreements often (perhaps usually) cut right across such artificial dividing lines. Thus it is not only possible, but also likely, that an intellectual representing a community that is notionally Christian may hold more doctrine-expressing sentences in common with a representative intellectual of a so-called Hindu community than with a representative intellectual belonging to another notionally Christian community. I, as an Anglican Christian, not infrequently find this to be my own case. There are, for example, Baptists with whom I find almost nothing in the way of intellectual common ground, just as there are Hindu theists with whom I find a very great deal. The adherents of esotericist perspectivalism make the recognition of this absolutely central to their view, and this is perhaps its strongest point.

Let us consider more closely, then, the empirical part of the thesis. Is it in fact the case that every religious community contains within it a small group of virtuosi (the first part of the esotericist perspectivalist's thesis)? And is it in fact the case that the experiences and teachings of these elites are always the same (the second part of the thesis)? The first part of the thesis seems broadly true. In the first chapter of this study I have suggested that religious communities typically have representative intellectuals, and these, certainly, are virtuosi of a kind. It is not, though, this kind of virtuoso that esotericists typically have in mind; the paradigm for them is not the intellectual, the analytically trained systematician. Rather, it is the mystic, the shaman, the prophet, the charismatic, the virtuoso of experience. This kind of virtuoso is not primarily concerned with formulating and defending sentences that express the doctrines of the community (although they may certainly also do this); rather, they embody, live out, and represent to the world the values and virtues of the community. They become its icon rather than its spokesperson. Such, for example, was Milarepa for Buddhists and Francis of Assisi for Christians. There seems no reason to doubt that religious communities typically do have such icons, no reason to doubt that they do have religious elites in the sense required by the adherent of esotericist perspectivalism.

The second part of the empirical thesis—that the experiences and teachings of these elites are always and everywhere the same—is more dubious. It expresses the esotericist perspectivalist's profound belief in the *philosophia perennis*, the perennial philosophy that is adhered to and taught by all religious virtuosi. Aldous Huxley, an esotericist if ever there was one, put it this way:

> *Philosophia perennis*—the phrase was coined by Leibniz; but the thing—the metaphysics that recognizes a divine Reality substantial to the world of things and lives and minds; the psychology that finds in the soul something similar to, or even identical with, divine Reality; the ethic that places man's final end in the knowledge of the immanent and transcendent Ground of all being—the thing is immemorial and universal. Rudiments of the Perennial Philosophy may be found among the traditionary lore of primitive peoples in every region of the world, and in its fully developed forms it has a place in every one of the higher religions. A version of this Highest Common Factor in all preceding and subsequent theologies was first committed to writing more than twenty-five centuries ago, and since that time the inexhaustible theme has been treated again and again, from the standpoint of every religious tradition and in all the principal languages of Asia and Europe.

This "Highest Common Factor," as Huxley puts it (notice the upper case letters), is the philosophy expressed in the teachings of these religious virtuosi; it is, according to esotericist perspectivalists, usually intimately connected with, and perhaps even directly expressive of, a universally available mystical experience. It is worth examining this thesis of the universality of (some kind of) mystical experience, since with it stands or falls the empirical part of the esotericist's thesis. In the discussion that follows I shall offer arguments that suggest that there is in fact no one single type of mystical experience, but rather (at least) three major types, and that the presumptive cognitive significance of each differs.

3.1 The Varieties of Mystical Experience

As yet, no generally agreed definition of mystical experience, or typology of varieties of mystical experience, has been arrived at. All scholars who have worked with the primary sources—largely texts—that describe the experiences that have come to be called "mystical" agree that it is not always clear that mystics from different traditions, or even different mystics from within the same tradition, are describing the same kind of experience. Some mystics use language suggestive of a loving and intimate relationship with another being; some use language that describes a feeling of unity with the physical universe; some speak of a complete transcendence of the space-time continuum; yet others of the realization that all distinctions are illusory and that ultimate reality is an undifferentiated unity. That such radical and apparently significant differences are to be found among the descriptions given by mystics to their experiences is uncontroversial.

From this uncontroversial fact about the records of mystical experience the following questions are immediately suggested. Is it possible to penetrate behind this array of significantly different descriptions of experiences to some more fundamental facts about these experiences that may enable us to describe their common core? Further, is there any hope for a useful classification of the types of mystical experience? In pursuing answers to these questions, I shall ask whether it is possible to distinguish the straightforward description of a given mystical experience from the culturally and doctrinally loaded interpretations given to it, either by its experiencer or by some later interpreter.

Some have answered this question in the negative and asserted that we cannot disentangle the phenomenological characteristics of a given mystical experience from the cultural and doctrinal matrix within which it came to expression, since the latter is a constitutive element of the former. If this position is taken, the necessary conclusion is that neither a crosscultural typology of mystical experience nor a description of the (putative) common core of all mystical experiences is possible. We can only say that there are as many types of mystical experiences as traditions within which they occur, or, even more despairingly, that there are as many types of mystical experiences as persons who have had them.

This last position is not only unnecessarily despairing; in its more extreme forms, it is also false. It is clear that we can penetrate behind the often highly interpreted descriptions of their experience given by mystics to the central phenomenological characteristics of those experiences, and that we can make necessarily imperfect but heuristically valuable attempts at describing those characteristics in tradition-neutral language. So, for example, it makes good sense to say that the mystical experience of both a Ramanuja and a Teresa of Avila exhibits many significant shared characteristics, and that few of these are apparent in the mystical experiences of a Shankara. It is possible, by the careful and sensitive use of phenomenological method, to penetrate behind the highly interpreted accounts of their experience left us by mystics to the central characteristics of those experiences themselves.

Given that this is possible, what is found when the attempt is made?

There are two widely held views. The first states that we find a common core, an essential element or elements common to all instances of genuine mystical experience. When stated in its strongest form, as it has frequently been by the prophets of hallucinogenic enlightenment, Zen-influenced Jesuits, proselytizing neo-Advaitins, gnomic Sufi masters, enlightened Tulkus, and ecumenically-minded philosophers of religion with a desire for world peace and international amity, this view amounts to the idea that mystical experience is always and everywhere the same, a *philosophia perennis* available to the spiritual elites of the world throughout history, differing only in insignificant incidentals — such as the terms in which it is expressed.

Opposed to this common-core view of mystical experience we find a range of semi-Wittgensteinean family resemblance views. Here the main claim is that a careful phenomenological examination of the records of mystical experience does not reveal any common core, and that instead we find "mystical experience" to be a label for a wide range of experiences that may share some characteristics, but which, in extreme cases, may have little or nothing in common with each other. Those who hold this view find it especially important to provide a classification of the types of mystical experience and a careful phenomenological description of their characteristics. It is clear, I think, that a careful reading of the descriptions we have of mystical experience suggests that this position is preferable.

Once it has been recognized that the records of mystical experience suggest that there is a wide range of types of such experience and that there is no easily recognizable common core, the next question that arises is that of the principle of classification to be used in developing a typology. The most fruitful approach is to attempt a classification of mystical experiences according to their phenomenological characteristics, that is, according to the object of the experience as it appears to its experiencer. An application of this criterion yields three basic types of mystical experience. Each may properly be further subdivided and classified, but a broad three-fold classification will do for the purposes of this study.

First, there is a range of experiences whose object is the material universe as a whole, and whose major characteristic is the appropriation of some previously unknown item(s) of information about the objects within this material universe. Such an item of information might be that there is a previously unperceived intimate link between the experiencer and the experienced, or that the apparent solidities and continuities perceptible in the material universe are not really there at all but are supplied by our constructive intellects, and that the universe is actually a series of causally connected point-instants. These experiences, and others like them, have as their phenomenological object the transfigured material universe. In them one directly perceives some previously unknown characteristic of that universe, and so these experiences are best classified as instances of nature mysticism; they are often hard to differentiate from the nature-ecstasy apparent in the poetry of the romantics. Wordsworth's "Lines Composed a Few Miles Above Tintern Abbey" represent much of what is important in this kind of mystical experience:

> . . . And I have felt
> A presence that disturbs me with the joy
> Of elevated thoughts; a sense sublime
> Of something far more deeply interfused,
> Whose dwelling is the light of setting suns,
> And the round ocean and the living air,
> And the blue sky, and in the mind of man.

Let us call this "nature mysticism."

Second, there is a range of experiences whose object is an external reality best characterized as personal, to be identified neither with the mystic's consciousness nor with the material universe. This, of course, is theistic mystical experience, and is relatively unproblematic in its phenomenological structure. Almost all descriptions of this type of experience use relational language, and in the overwhelming majority of cases the imagery and symbols of human love—often sexual love—are found most appropriate. This type of experience, then, is phenomenologically quite distinct from the types of nature mysticism briefly described in the preceding paragraph; it is best described as an intimate and loving relationship with a benevolent other. Let us call this "theistic mysticism."

Third, there is a type of experience that is truly introvertive in that it has itself as an object: this is an experience of pure, empty consciousness, without phenomenological structure, and without any object other than itself. Let us call this "monistic mysticism." It is significantly different from both nature mysticism and theistic mystical experience in its presumptive cognitive significance, since it seems to be more akin to self-referential experiences such as being in pain than it is to normal sensory experience, which is typically structured by the division between subject and object. I shall return to the question of cognitive significance in a moment.

While it has been given only the briefest of sketches here, I consider this threefold classification of mystical experience to be broadly adequate to the historical record of the experiences of mystics in diverse traditions, and to further reflect the inescapable fact that mystical experience is in no interesting sense always and everywhere the same. A full and detailed support of this typology would require the analysis of many examples, an enterprise that cannot be entered into here. Its adequacy will have to be taken on trust. Its acceptance, though, has very important consequences for any discussion of the cognitive value of mystical experience, and since esotericist perspectivalists typically claim that the mystical experience of religious elites is veridical, I must now turn to this question.

3.2 The Cognitive Value of the Varieties of Mystical Experience

To consider the presumptive cognitive value of theistic mystical experience first: there appear to be significant analogies between ordinary sensory experience and this kind of mystical experience. Both are noetic in the sense that they have a (real or imagined) object, and this object is typically experienced as other than the observer. Further, both lead to the making of claims about something other than the experience, and for both independent tests are necessary and available for the checking of such claims.

Examples may make this clearer. As an example of a sensory experience, consider the experience of seeming to see a duck-billed platypus; as an example of theistic mystical experience, consider the beatific vision, in which one seems to directly experience an intimate and loving union with a benevolent and transcendent personal other. Clearly, both have an object—in the one case the duck-billed platypus and in the other God—which is experienced as other than the observer. Also, both lead to the making of claims about something other than the observer, namely, *a duck-billed platypus exists* and *a benevolent and personal God exists*. Further, these claims are subject to test and theoretical falsification. If, for example, a claim is contradictory, or along with other propositions known to be true entails a contradiction, then it must be false. If someone, on the basis of a platypus experience, claims that the platypus in question was dancing a square circle, then there are good grounds for rejecting the claim; likewise for the claim that a benevolent and personal God exists if it can be shown, for example, that this claim contradicts the well-grounded proposition that there is a lot of evil in the world.

Once it is established that the claims derived from our paradigm cases of sensory experience and theistic mystical experience are not contradictory or otherwise incoherent, or, what is the same, that it is logically possible to see a platypus and to encounter a living personal God, the next series of tests runs something like this. Is the experience from which the relevant claim is derived likely to be a genuine or deceptive instance of the class of (logically possible) experiences to which it belongs? For example, in the large class of logically possible duck-billed platypus experiences, is a particular proposition, such as *a duck-billed platypus climbed the Capitol steps this morning* likely to refer to a veridical experience or to a deceptive one? Relevant considerations here are whether the specific experience upon which the proposition is based shares the characteristics of such experiences in general. That is, did the putative platypus possess the distinguishing features of a platypus as opposed to (say) a raccoon or a beaver? Was it seen on the Capitol steps by other persons at the relevant time? Should it have been? Is there any reason to question the honesty of persons who claim to have seen the platypus? Is there any reason to question the reliability of their perceptual faculties at the time of the putative platypus-experience? If these and similar questions are answered properly, then we are likely to regard the sensory experience in question as veridical.

The approach to theistic mystical experience within a believing community is essentially the same. Accepting that the putative object of the experience exists, and that there are guidelines available that define the features proper to a theistic mystical experience, the person who claims to have had such an experience can be asked similar sorts of questions. For example: Did the being with whom you claim to have experienced intimate and loving union exhibit those characteristics attributed to him by others who have had this experience? Has your conduct been altered for the better by this experience? And so on. Here, of course, tests for the veridicality of theistic mystical experience developed within traditions for which such experience is of fundamental importance are being applied. The existence of such tests provides no independent reason for accepting the veridicality of the experience to which they apply; but it does provide further support for the affirmation of a close analogy between theistic mystical experience and sensory experience.

At this point, to reinforce my contention that monistic and theistic mystical experiences differ at almost every level, it needs to be pointed out that no such independent tests can be suggested for the "veridicality" of a given instance of monistic mystical experience. The reason for this is that monistic mystical experience lacks the intentional structure that gives such tests their rationale in the case of both theistic mystical experience and sensory experience; instead, monistic mystical experience, like subjective feeling states, is incorrigible. It makes no sense to ask whether a given instance of feeling pain is veridical or not; the experience carries its own guarantee. It makes no sense to ask those who claim to be in pain whether they are really in pain or whether they might merely seem to be in pain but actually are mistaken. As a result, the interpretation of a pain experience is logically independent of its content (consider the pains "in" the missing limbs of amputees). So also with monistic mystical experience. It may very well be that monistic mystical experience is a cosmic morning sickness pregnant with ontological implications; but there is nothing about its phenomenology that requires or even suggests that this is so. The interpretation of a monistic mystical experience is logically independent of its content (if indeed it has any), whereas the interpretation of a theistic mystical experience must begin with its content.

The case is different again with nature mysticism. There is no directly specifiable object of such experience in the same way that there is for theistic mystical experience. Instead, as I have suggested, the object of nature-mystical experiences is the whole of the material universe. Whereas theistic mystical experience is like meeting a person of whose existence we were previously unaware, nature mysticism is like suddenly perceiving that every object we have ever had contact with, appearances notwithstanding, is actually made of green cheese in a wide variety of disguises.

Clearly this second type of experience, the green cheese experience, is not very much like sensory experience. It may be cued by various types of sensory experience, but does not itself have a very strong structural analogy with such experience. A better model for understanding this type of mystical experience would seem to be that of intuitive problem solving. The data do not change; our understanding of them does. Thus we may watch a chess match between two grandmasters for an hour, seeing each move as it is made, studying the changing configurations of the pieces, but only with the twentieth move suddenly understanding the long-term strategy that underlay each preceding move. Nothing has changed with regard to the sensory input, but at the moment when we suddenly understand the strategy underlying the configuration of the chess pieces, we learn something we did not know before. So also with the green cheese experience. The sense data do not change: objects still have varying shapes, colors, and textures, but we suddenly realize that in fact they are all made of green cheese. Afficionados of Zen literature will realize that *satori* is often described in just such terms, and it is arguable that the fundamental insight described in Indian Buddhist literature is also best understood on this model.

Intuitive understanding that transforms our perception of the totality of events in a given situation — or, in the case of nature mysticism, the totality of events in the entire material universe — is capable of being true or false, accurate or inaccurate. Thus I may correctly intuit the chess master's strategy or completely misunderstand it; the objects in the material universe really may be made of green cheese or they may not. And so on. The type of intuitive understanding under discussion here carries with it no guarantees of accuracy. Just as with sensory perception, further tests are needed, though they are rather different in kind.

These questions enter a difficult realm: What constitutes a good explanation of a given set of data, and how does one distinguish between two rival explanations in terms of their adequacy? This is a notoriously difficult issue and one of central importance in the philosophy of science. Assuming that the intuitive understanding arrived at in any given instance is not self-contradictory or incoherent, and further assuming that it is not easily falsified by empirical data, imponderables such as the explanatory power of the view under consideration, whether it covers all instances of the data to which it relates, and whether it harmonizes with well-established hypotheses in other areas, have to be considered. This is a complex task, though by no means an impossible one. It is quite beyond the scope of the present study.

If this analysis of mystical experience and its types stands, the empirical part of the esotericist perspectivalist's thesis will not. There is a further reason why the latter should be rejected: it almost always presupposes an unconsidered dichotomy between religious experience and doctrinal expression, of a kind similar to that held by the experiential expressivist. For the esotericist perspectivalist, as much as for the experiential expressivist, religious experience is always prior to and determinative of its expression in doctrine-expressing sentences. I have offered arguments for thinking this to be false in 2.2 above, in my discussion of experiential expressivism, and will not repeat them here.

Now clearly, if the empirical part of esotericist perspectivalism is to be rejected, its normative part cannot be straightforwardly accepted. For if there is a range of types of mystical experience, and if the doctrines enunciated by religious virtuosi are not always and everywhere the same, it cannot be the case that all mystical experiences are veridical and all doctrine-expressing sentences true. If the profoundly personal theistic mysticism of Teresa of Avila is veridical and the doctrine-expressing sentences that both formed it and express it are true, then a Zen Buddhist's *satori* cannot be veridical, and the doctrine-expressing sentences that both form and express it cannot be true. The normative part of the esotericist perspectivalist's position thus has to be restated if it is to stand at all. It becomes something like: *one of the modalities of the experiences typically had by religious virtuosi is veridical and one of the sets of sentences that shapes this kind of experience and expresses its implications is true.* And with this there is no problem, since it puts esotericist perspectivalists right back into the apologetical arena where they properly belong: argument for the veridicality of the favored type of experience and the truth of the favored set of sentences becomes unavoidable, just as it also does for the universalist.

The conclusion to be drawn from the positions discussed in this chapter is that while the varieties of perspectivalism have their strengths, there is no reason to think that their central contentions are true, and many reasons to think that they are not. The possibility that doctrine-expressing sentences of different religious communities might be incompatible one with another is thus not ruled out by the arguments offered by adherents of perspectivalism, and, as I have shown, there is a good deal of prima facie evidence to suggest that such incompatibility is instanced.

4

The Rejection of Positive Apologetics

The NOIA principle claims that when intellectuals representing a certain religious community judge that there is a significant incompatibility between their doctrine-expressing sentences and those of some other religious community, they have an ethical and epistemic duty to engage in both positive and negative apologetics. If the arguments offered in chapters 2 and 3 are good, there is no reason to reject this claim on the grounds that the doctrine-expressing sentences of religious communities have no cognitive content, or on the ground that they do not or cannot conflict with one another. But there are those, some in very influential positions in theological academies, who would agree with all, or virtually all, of the arguments offered in chapters 2 and 3 of this study, and yet who would reject positive apologetics tout court, even while allowing negative apologetics.

Recall that negative apologetics consists in a series of defensive manoeuvres through which a given community defends its doctrines from external attack. Through positive apologetics, by contrast, the community attempts more: it tries to show that its doctrines are superior, cognitively, epistemically, or ethically, to those of competing religious communities. Why, then, might some intellectuals want to allow negative apologetics but disallow positive apologetics?

4.1 THE ARGUMENT FROM NEGATIVE EFFECT

This argument needs comparatively little time and effort, since it is neither particularly sophisticated not particularly difficult to demolish. One who rejects engagement in positive apologetics for this reason claims simply that the negative effects of engaging in it are so great as to make it always undesirable. For example: suppppose a Buddhist intellectual holds to the doctrine-expressing sentence *the claim that there exists an eternal, uncaused, omniscient, omnipotent being who desires the welfare of the entire human race is both internally incoherent and produces undesirable effects in those who assent to it.* Assent to this doctrine-expressing sentence, if taken seriously, entails that the doctrine-expressing sentence of (some) Christian communities, *there exists an eternal, uncaused, omniscient being who desires the welfare of the entire human race,* must be false. Our Buddhist intellectual might well realize this, might well judge that both his doctrine-expressing sentence and its Christian contradictory have cognitive content, with the important difference that his is true and the Christian intellectual's false, and might yet abstain from positive apologetics, because he judges that engaging in it will necessarily produce anguish, antagonism, religious hatred, doubt, and perhaps even violence. The present Dalai Lama, Tenzin Gyatso, expressed this view clearly in a lecture on religious harmony given at a number of venues during his tour of North America in 1981:

> Among spiritual faiths, there are many different philosophies, some just opposite to each other on certain points. Buddhists do not accept a creator; Christians base their philosophy on that theory. There are great differences . . . if we go into the differences in philosophy and argue with and criticize each other, it is useless. There will be endless argument; the result will mainly be that we irritate each other — accomplishing nothing. Better to look at the purpose of the philosophies and to see what is shared.

No doubt it has often been the case that little but irritation has been produced by engagement in positive apologetics. Sincere and passionate religious believers typically tend to be unhappy if they are told that from the viewpoint of another religious community some key doctrine-expressing sentences in which they believe are self-evidently false. They may indeed react with irritation or worse; one of the effects of the tendency toward absoluteness possessed by the doctrine-expressing sentences of many religious communities is just that when these doctrine-expressing sentences are called into question by an outsider, and when that questioning is taken seriously by one who assents to them, the result is often a profound anxiety, uneasiness, and fear. Those in such a condition will often lash out at what threatens. Hence the Dalai Lama's fears. Hence also, I suspect, the unchallenging nature of much of today's interreligious dialogue.

Buddhists have erected this realization into a principle that has direct application to the question that concerns me in this chapter. The principle is that of *upayakaushalya,* "skill in proper salvific methods," a skill that is possessed to perfection by Buddhas, but which is also set up as a goal for all Buddhists. One who exercises skill in proper salvific methods is able to see that different situations require different modes of action; that what one says must be pitched at the level of one's hearers if one is to be understood; and that the primary consideration in deciding whether to engage in one course of action or another must be the effects of that action on those at whom it is directed. Such a principle is not centrally concerned with truth; it is pragmatic. Telling lies is not only permissible but required, if doing so will help one's hearer toward Nirvana. Engagement in positive apologetics will then be regarded as desirable only if it also seems that it might help those at whom it is aimed to approach more closely to that condition of dispassionate compassion toward which Buddhist soteriology ultimately points all human beings. In order to be helped in this way by having a positive apologetic aimed at one, one would presumably have to be obsessively entangled in false intellectual views. Since, according to standard issue Buddhist diagnoses of the human condition, that is the condition in which most of us are mired, it is perhaps not surprising that Buddhist intellectuals have, traditionally, engaged in a wide variety of intellectual practices that fit very appropriately under the heading of positive apologetics.

I suspect that the Dalai Lama's employment of the argument from negative effect springs not so much from an application of the principle of skill in proper salvific methods as from the tenuous situation of the Tibetan people and the dubious prospects for the restoration of Tibetan political autonomy. This, if it is correct, raises the issue of the proper political conditions for the use of positive apologetics, an important question to which I shall return in chapter 5.

More generally, it is hard to see that the argument from negative effect points to anything but a contingent truth about the behavior and reactions of a significantly large sample of religious believers. It is hard to see it as a logical truth of any kind: there are no obvious reasons why those who assent to doctrine-expressing sentences *must* react in this way. Other reactions are possible, and indeed required by the presuppositions of at least some religious communities. Many Christians would argue that true faith never responds to challenges from outside with violence, nor even with irritation. For many Buddhists, an encounter with positive apologetics should be an occasion for the exercise of *karuna*, of compassion, not for religous hatred. So there are resources available within religious communities that can be used to deal with the natural, though reprehensible, tendency of committed religious human beings to react negatively to an encounter with positive apologetics aimed at their own doctrine-expressing sentences. These resources can and should be mobilized by the representative intellectuals of religious communities. If this were done, many of the Dalai Lama's fears could at least be alleviated, and perhaps removed altogether.

There is a further point to be made. Arguments for the superiority of one religious community's doctrine-expressing sentences over those of another rarely (perhaps never) take place in an institutional vacuum. That is to say, such arguments have, historically, rarely been separated from situations in which there are more than purely intellectual or even purely soteriological issues at stake. It is one thing for a Christian to argue that some doctrine-expressing sentences assented to by some Jews are false within the bounds of the academy in a culture like that of the USA, in which the danger of such arguments being translated into real political action against Jews is remote. It is quite another to engage in such arguments in a situation in which those whose doctrine-expressing sentences are being argued against are under political, military, or any other kind of external pressure by those doing the arguing. Argument in a situation of this kind is not innocent and can often be an instrument in the service of oppression. And it is probably true that positive apologetics has been so used in the past. But, once again, this is not a necessary concomitant of engagement in positive apologetics, and is not a sufficient reason for rejecting, in a priori fashion, its use.

Recall the arguments offered against universalist perspectivalism in 3.1 above. Here, as there, I would assert that the empirical observation that positive apologetics has often been used in the service of oppression cannot be used as a blanket argument against its desirability, any more than the fact that every technological innovation brings with it a concomitant possibility (usually actualized) for military application to be used as a blanket argument against the desirability of technological research. I shall return to these points when, in chapter 5, I briefly set forth the conditions under which a proper positive apologetic can be undertaken. I conclude here that the argument from negative effect, while empirically not without strength, has little or no logical force; also, when it is realized, as it usually is not by proponents of the argument from negative effect, that there are genuine positive results to be reaped by all concerned from the proper application of positive apologetics, the argument becomes even less convincing. It can, though, serve as a useful reminder that apologetics must, to the extent possible, be divorced from the threat, implicit or explicit, of military, socioeconomic, or cultural oppression.

4.2 THE ARGUMENT THAT SUCCESS IS IMPOSSIBLE

Many theological thinkers regard positive apologetics as a branch of natural theology. This seems quite proper; if we think of natural theology as the branch of theological thought that operates independently of revelation by the application of unaided human reason to the solution of difficult theological and other intellectual problems, then positive apologetics quite clearly belongs to it. Positive apologetics, as defined briefly in chapter 1 of this study, is a discourse that uses only methods of argumentation and criteria of knowledge that are acceptable to the adversary. This limitation was designed to rule out appeals to sources of revelation not accepted by those beyond the bounds of the religious community engaging in positive apologetics; its inclusion makes it very clear that positive apologetics is a branch of natural theology in the usual sense of that term.

There are some theological thinkers, most especially perhaps those working within the intellectual tradition that looks to John Calvin as its founding father, who would reject positive apologetics just because it is a branch of natural theology. It is notorious that Calvin had rather little time for natural theology—and thus also for positive apologetics—and the same appears true for some of his intellectual heirs in the Reformed tradition. One of the arguments offered against natural theology by thinkers from this tradition is that the standards for a successful piece of positive apologetics are impossibly high: it just cannot be done. Or so it is said.

Why might this be thought? I suspect that such a position is held because of a reliance upon an inappropriate model of what an argument in positive apologetics should look like. The claim that it cannot be done, that is to say, rests upon an intuition that if it could be done, we would have access to a series of neat, tight, precise, and utterly convincing deductive arguments whose premises would be agreed upon as true by all sane human beings, and whose conclusions would follow necessarily from those premises.

If this model is to be followed, the Dalai Lama would, in order to engage in successful positive apologetics against the doctrine-expressing sentences of some Christian community that stand in contradiction with those espoused by Gelukpa Buddhists, have to produce a knockdown drag-out deductive argument for the truth of some doctrine-expressing sentence, such as *no existent has any accidental properties* (which would entail the falsity of most Christian affirmations about God), or (still more difficult) *any sentence that predicates any property of any existent is false because it can be shown to entail some contradiction.* Or, to look at the other side of the case, Christian theologians in at least some communities would need to be able to offer just such arguments for the truth of doctrine-expressing sentences, such as *God is a necessarily existent being* or *God is atemporal yet can act in time*, since the truth of these sentences would entail the falsity of many Gelukpa Buddhist claims. Now, obviously, this cannot be done. There are no such arguments. Or if there are, no one has yet discovered them. And in this limited sense the intuition that the standards for a successful piece of positive apologetics are impossibly high has some validity.

But there is no need to accept these standards. There is no reason whatever to accept the paradigm of the knockdown drag-out argument as appropriate for a successful piece of positive apologetics. A much more appropriate paradigm is that of the cumulative-case argument, in which the apologist attempts to show the cognitive superiority of the system formed by the doctrine-expressing sentences of one religious community over that formed by those of another by a complex and related series of arguments, no one of which is individually decisive. For example: the doctrine-expressing sentences isolated and stated in the preceding paragraph have their life and power as elements within a much broader and more complex set of doctrine-expressing sentences. Those of the Gelukpa Buddhist operate as part of a radical critique of the possibilities of discursive reason, a critique that calls into question the possibility of making claims to truth at all, and which assumes as basic a complex and well-developed Buddhist critique of all substance-attribute ontologies. All of this would have to be taken into account by a Buddhist from this tradition wishing to engage in successful positive apologetics against the doctrine-expressing sentences asserted by some rival religious community.

Given the ontological and linguistic presuppositions of the Gelukpa system (for system it is, even if its adherents prefer not to call it such), one tends to find, as one would expect, that when adherents of the tradition do engage in apologetics (and, historically, they often have), they do so by offering a series of linked arguments that severally attempt to show that opposing positions are prima facie incoherent or necessarily issue in incoherence through the application to them of basic principles of the predicate calculus; and which jointly issue in the conclusion that all sets of doctrine-expressing sentences are cognitively inferior to that espoused by Gelukpa Buddhists, because all of them issue in conceptual incoherence and that of the Gelukpas alone does not.

It may seem as though this approach to apologetics, consisting as it does in the attempt to show that an opposing set of doctrine-expressing sentences either is incoherent or that it issues in incoherence if pressed, should properly be classified as negative rather than positive apologetics. It may appear that this method does not attempt to demonstrate the superiority of its own set of doctrine-expressing sentences, but rather to show that there is some pressing conceptual problem inherent in all others, and thus that every other fails in its challenge to the Gelukpa position. This appearance, though, is misleading, and issues from the rather unusual doctrinal position of the Gelukpa. Since that school claims to hold no affirmative philosophical thesis (*pratijña* or *drishti*) of its own (I shall not discuss here the difficulties inherent in the claim that holding no affirmative thesis of one's own is not itself an affirmative thesis), the only method left open to its adherents for the demonstration of the superiority of the school's (non)position is to argue that all other positions are internally incoherent, so leaving the Gelukpa as the only contender still in the field. Thus even the extreme case of the Gelukpa (and, before it in India, the Madhyamika) attempt to demolish all other philosophical positions can, given its context, properly be understood as an example of cumulative-case positive apologetics.

Christian, Jewish, and Islamic versions of cumulative-case apologetics are much more familiar. They typically offer a series of linked, probabilistic, inductive arguments for the truth of key doctrine-expressing sentences—such, for instance, as the sentence *the cosmos was created in its entirety by God*—which issue in conclusions such as *it is more probable than not that the cosmos was created in its entirety by God,* or *it is more probable that the cosmos was created in its entirety by God than that any other hypothesis about the origins of the cosmos is true.* Classic instances of arguments of this kind are plentiful in all three traditions.

Once again, it is not my goal here to assess the success of any given example of cumulative-case positive apologetics. I want to offer a defense only of the formal point that successful pursuit of the goals inherent in such an intellectual discourse is not logically impossible. It will, of course, be very difficult to judge in any given case whether and to what extent an instance of cumulative-case positive apologetics has been successful. To do so will almost always involve nothing short of assessing the convincingness of an entire metaphysic, cosmology, and ontology. But there is no reason to suppose that such an enterprise is impossible — not, at least, without trying it. To put the point as sharply as possible: if positive apologetics (understood as I have defined it) is to be judged undesirable, because it can never be brought to a successful conclusion, such a judgement would involve something like the following claim: *it is theoretically impossible to demonstrate the cognitive superiority of one ordered set of doctrine-expressing sentences over another.* And this, to put it mildly, is massively implausible unless one adopts a noncognitive reading of doctrine-expressing sentences like those discussed in chapter 2.

Consider, as a counterexample to this claim, the case of an ordered set of doctrine-expressing sentences that includes among its members *the establishment of a racially pure society is the highest religious value* and *the use of genocide in the service of this goal is desirable.* Perhaps some quasi-Christians in Nazi Germany might have assented to both of these doctrine-expressing sentences. If they are to be defensible it would seem that the following must be true: *there must be some way of discriminating the racially pure from the impure.* For if this is not true, the set of doctrine-expressing sentences in question labors under the unfortunate debility of being quite incapable of being put into practice. One would not know at whom to direct one's genocidal efforts if one did not know who was racially pure and who was not. Consider now the positive apologetic that might be developed against this set of doctrine-expressing sentences by a holder of some opposed set of doctrine-expressing sentences that includes the following: *interracial harmony is a significant religious value* and *any group that encourages racial divisiveness is, on religious grounds, to be acted against.* Many religious communities would, I think, assent to something closely analogous to these two doctrine-expressing sentences. And all those who do are placed under an ethico-religious imperative to engage in positive apologetics against the racist religious communities postulated.

One way in which this might be done (and there are many other possibilities) would be to develop a linked set of arguments surrounding the very idea of racial purity and impurity. If one could begin to show, through arguments based upon genetics, history, and so forth, that the concept is internally flawed, an idea that has no roots in the realities of the human condition, one would have begun to show that the doctrine-expressing sentences of the nonracist religious community are cognitively superior to those of the racist community. One might then continue to develop a quasi-

Kantian metaethic to argue for the truth of the nonracist set of doctrine-expressing sentences, and to show that the first-order ethic entailed by assent to the doctrine-expressing sentences of the racist religious community is indefensible on the basis of such a metaethic—and so forth.

My purpose in mentioning this example is not to develop a full-blown positive apologetic in favor of the set of doctrine-expressing sentences that advocates racial harmony over that which advocates genocide as a tool for realizing religious value. To do that would require a large volume to itself. I use the example (admittedly an extreme case) only to suggest that there is no reason to suppose that cumulative-case positive apologetics is necessarily an enterprise for which the standards are impossibly high. Those who object to positive apologetics—and also to natural theology—on such a ground tend to do so only because they have in mind as a paradigm of success the isolated deductive argument, an argument whose truth is self-evident and the truth of whose premises one cannot preserve sanity and deny. Arguments of this kind are rare in any setting, and perhaps especially rare in any interesting setting such as that constituted by theological discourse. But this fact by itself does nothing to call into question the viability of positive apologetics in the sense given to that term in this study.

Finally, it is obviously true that success in positive apologetics is impossible if by that one means the transmission of a specific religious conviction by argument to all those who do not now possess it. Human irrationality is too deeply rooted for that to be a realistic hope. Some still believe that the earth is flat; but this says nothing as to whether there are or are not decent arguments to show the cognitive superiority of the belief that it is an oblate spheroid. So also, mutatis mutandis, for the existence of God. To acknowledge that most human beings are not moved by rational considerations, and that such considerations play little part in the religious lives of most men and women, is to do more than to acknowledge that apologetics, positive or negative, plays only a small part in the theological enterprise. It is no less important for that.

4.3 THE ARGUMENT THAT POSITIVE APOLOGETICS IS UNNECESSARY FOR THE PRESERVATION OF EPISTEMIC RESPECTABILITY

It is often said, especially by Reformed theologians, that religious believers may be epistemically justified in assenting to some or all of the central doctrine-expressing sentences of their religious community even if they are unable to construct demonstrative (or any other) arguments for their truth. This objection, which is both more powerful and more interesting than that discussed in the previous section, calls into question the necessity of positive apologetics (though not of negative apologetics) in an interesting way. It claims that believers can fulfill all their epistemic obligations without having to engage in the enterprise of trying to show that their beliefs are cognitively superior to those competitors of which they happen to be aware.

What, then, does it mean to have epistemic obligations, duties in regard to the beliefs to which one assents, and how might one violate such obligations? This is an enormously complex subject, a full treatment of which would require the development of a comprehensive epistemological theory. Here I can do no more than offer a somewhat simplistic account.

Let me first introduce a basic axiom: every human being is placed under the epistemic obligation to avoid knowing assent to false propositions. To engage in such assent is, of course, a form of (psychologically odd) falsehood, primarily to oneself but usually also to others. If one assents to the claim *the planet earth is not more than six thousand years old* while knowing this claim to be false, one is (apart from being in a very odd psychological condition: What can it mean to assent to a claim that one knows to be false?) a liar. One is such even if one's assent remains an entirely private matter. Such knowing assent to false propositions thus violates one, perhaps the most basic, of one's epistemic obligations.

There are various ways of extending this obligation, none of them entirely unproblematic. One might argue that one has an obligation to maximize one's stock of true beliefs and minimize one's stock of false beliefs. But this leads to the conclusion that human beings must eternally be trying to discover more true beliefs to which they can assent, a fate, like that of Sisyphus, which is not to be envied. More reasonably, one might argue that it is a basic epistemic duty to reconsider any specific belief that one has when one meets a significant challenge to it. This brings us close to the kind of situation envisaged by the NOIA principle. But even this requirement seems too stringent to be universalized. For there are always, or almost always, actual challenges to every belief that one holds, religious or other, and if each and all human beings are epistemically required to reconsider each belief to which they become aware that there is a challenge of some kind, life would consist of nothing else but a continual reassessment of one's beliefs. And this is not a very promising basis upon which to function as a religious believer. It would seem, then, that only certain kinds of challenges to one's beliefs require the kind of reassessment described, and it turns out to be exceedingly difficult to specify precisely the conditions that must be met by a challenge in order for it to be the kind that should force a reassessment.

Let us consider an extreme case. Suppose you hold the belief that *all members of religious communities other than my own are engaged in the devil's work*, and suppose further that your sole ground for holding this belief is that you have had a vision of a religiously significant supernatural being who has told you that this is the case. Suppose further that you have discovered that all the beliefs you have come to hold in the past on this basis are false; imagine that last week the very same supernatural being appeared in a vision and told you that you would learn, within two days, that you are to be audited by the Internal Revenue Service, and that this did not happen;

and suppose that you have experienced many other instances of this kind. Suppose, yet further, that you have real and pressing empirical evidence that there is something wrong with the belief adverted to — for example, that all the members of religious communities other than your own whom you happen to meet appear, on the face of things, to be intensely concerned for your welfare, and to spend all their time pressing material and spiritual blessings upon you. Suppose, finally, that your belief is specifically challenged by a representative intellectual of another religious community, who argues to your face that all sincere religious practitioners are serving God and are therefore not engaged in the devil's work.

In such a case, you know that you have come to hold your belief on the basis of an unreliable belief-forming mechanism, for everything you have been told in your visions up to this point has turned out to be false; you have some empirical evidence that the specific belief in question is false; and you are faced with a specific challenge to your belief by a holder of a belief that, if true, entails the falsity of your belief. This is an extreme case and was constructed to serve as such: it is intended to suggest that in some cases one has a clear epistemic duty to reassess religious beliefs that one holds, for surely no one would doubt that individuals in this situation would not be fulfilling all their epistemic duties were they to continue to hold the belief that *all members of religious communities other than my own are engaged in the devil's work.*

In such an extreme case, how might apologetics, of both the positive and negative kind, fit into the picture? How might engagement in these forms of discourse help beleaguered religious believers, and can they discharge their epistemic duties in this situation without entering into positive apologetics? They might, of course, attempt to discharge these duties solely by applying negative apologetics. This would amount simply to an attempt to show that, even though the evidence against their belief is very pressing, it is not decisive; they may still be holding a true belief, it might be argued, just as long as they can show that it is not logically impossible that their belief is true, and they can therefore claim to be noetically justified — to have fulfilled all their epistemic obligations — without entering into attempts to show that their view is cognitively superior to its competitors.

However, in an extreme case like that mentioned, such a position sounds somewhat implausible. To show that one (logically) may be holding a true belief does not suffice in cases of extreme epistemic pressure; not only the publicans and tax collectors, but also the racists and the flat earthers can do as much. While it is going to be difficult, perhaps impossible (for we have no access to an epistemic calculus of the proper kind) to decide in any given case whether and to what extent positive apologetics will be required for a given individual, it is surely not difficult to see that it is required in some cases. To state the situation abstractly: one of one's epistemic obligations is to engage in positive apologetics in situations wherein it appears that the reasons for holding the contradictory of what one holds are strong and pressing. In such a situation one ought (epistemically) to try to construct arguments for the cognitive superiority of one's position to some one or more of the competitors who are creating the situation of epistemic pressure; only by so doing will one succeed in discharging one's epistemic obligations. It is one of the burdens of the NOIA principle to suggest that on some occasions the awareness on the part of some representative intellectuals of some particular religious community that their opposite numbers in some other religious community hold to doctrine-expressing sentences incompatible with their own creates just such a situation.

A caveat needs to be entered here. The NOIA principle might, perhaps, be understood to mean that, in the case of Buddhists, all Buddhists, however unlettered, unlearned, and unsophisticated, are required to engage in positive apologetics as soon as they become aware that many Christians seem to assert doctrine-expressing sentences that are incompatible with their own. Such a conclusion is not intended, principally because one of the variables to be taken into account in coming to a decision as to whether the NOIA principle applies to the case of a particular religious believer is the intellectual capacity of that believer. Many sincere religious believers in all religious communities simply lack the intellectual capacity to construct arguments in support of any of their beliefs, or even to bring their beliefs to full awareness, much less to enter upon the very demanding discipline of positive apologetics. When such is the case, it would surely be an undue and improper burden upon the belief-forming and belief-maintenance practices of such individuals to require that they engage in an intellectual practice for which they are not equipped.

This does not (or does not necessarily) mean, though, that such persons are not discharging their epistemic obligations in virtue of incapacity; they may be fulfilling these obligations in virtue of being members of a religious community in which there are representative intellectuals who do engage in positive apologetics in the kind of situation envisaged by the NOIA principle. It was, as I have already mentioned in the course of the brief outline of the NOIA principle given in chapter 1, partly in order to avoid placing an improper burden upon the belief-forming and belief-maintenance practices of the unlearned that the principle was framed in terms of the duties of representative intellectuals of religious communities, and not in terms of the epistemic obligations of the individual believer. I note parenthetically here that those who argue most strongly for the position that religious believers can fulfill all their epistemic obligations without entering into positive apologetics tend to come from traditions that emphasize the individual at the expense of the community. A community may have epistemic duties that need not be fulfilled by every individual member of it; and this too is a point not often adverted to by those who argue that epistemic and ethical obligations can always be fulfilled without positive apologetics.

I conclude that there are situations in which it is not possible for a religious community to fulfil its epistemic duties without entering into positive apologetics, and I suggest that the situation envisaged by the NOIA principle is a paradigm case of such. This is because, in such a situation, a religious community is typically presented with the realization that its own absolute answers to the mysteries of human existence and human salvation are directly challenged by an incompatible set of answers given by another community, and that, typically, this opposed set of answers provides an existence apparently just as meaningful and ordered for its adherents as does the set adhered to by the members of the first religious community for its.

The realization that there is every appearance that some other religious community's set of doctrine-expressing sentences is, formally and functionally, on a par with one's own both should and usually does create just the kind of epistemic pressure that concerns me. Even for those who are members of religious communities whose doctrine-expressing sentences are guaranteed for them by some powerful community-specific source of authority — such as an inerrant sacred text or authority figure — awareness of other religious communities with other doctrine-expressing sentences and other community-specific sources of authority will often create a profound epistemic uneasiness. And it is to this situation that the NOIA principle is addressed.

So much for the objection that one can preserve epistemic respectability without engaging in positive apologetics: some individual religious believers may indeed always be able to do so, but I think that no religious community can rely on being always in such a situation, especially now that a direct and continuous experience of religious pluralism is an increasingly important part of the life of most religious communities. It is relevant at this point to spend a little time on the interesting case of the Great Pumpkin.

4.3.1 An Excursus on the Case of the Pumpkinites

Imagine a religious community whose central belief is: *there is a Great Pumpkin who returns to the pumpkin-patch every Hallowe'en to save our souls.* Imagine further that the representative intellectuals of this (small) religious community are relatively sophisticated thinkers who would allow most of the presuppositions operative in the NOIA principle. They would allow, that is, that religious communities typically do construct and assert sentences in natural languages that they take to express their doctrines; that these sentences typically do have a cognitive dimension; that it is possible for the claims to knowledge contained in the doctrine-expressing sentences of one religious community to be genuinely incompatible with those of another; and that such incompatibility is sometimes actually met with. The representative intellectuals of the Pumpkinite community further think it incumbent upon them to defend their doctrine-expressing sentences against those who claim to be able to show that they must be false or that it is irrational to believe in them. They thus frequently exercise their philosophical wits by engaging in negative apologetics, for they find that there are many non-Pumpkinites only too ready to try to show that Pumpkinite doctrines are absurd and should be assented to by no reasonable human being.

But the representative intellectuals of the Pumpkinites do not wish to engage in positive apologetics. They have no desire whatever to convince non-Pumpkinites that Pumpkinite doctrines are cognitively superior in any sense to those of (say) Mahayana Buddhism. And they are free from such desires because they think their epistemic duties fulfilled when they have established that there is neither prima facie incoherence in their own doctrine-expressing sentences and what they entail, nor irrationality in assenting to them. Further, being sophisticated, those intellectuals who represent the Pumpkinites want to claim more than simply that they are not offending against any epistemic duties in holding the beliefs they hold: they want to claim that they *know* that what is expressed in their doctrine-expressing sentences is true. They know that *there is a Great Pumpkin who returns to the pumpkin patch every Hallowe'en to save our souls*, and they know this without having to produce (and even without having) proof for its truth, and, just as importantly, without this knowledge being based upon any evidence or any chain of reasoning, or indeed upon anything else whatever. Consider the following way of putting this view:

> Indeed on the Pumpkinite tradition in question, the proposition that there is such a person as the Great Pumpkin belongs itself to the foundational level of knowledge. It is a proposition that believers (many of them, at any rate) know *immediately*. According to this tradition, the most appropriate way to believe in the Great Pumpkin is not to believe on the basis of evidence or argument from other propositions, but to take this belief—that there is such a person as the Great Pumpkin—as basic. One who does so, furthermore, typically *knows* that there is such a person as the Great Pumpkin, even if he or she can't show and doesn't even try to show that it can be proved by reference to what is self-evident and incorrigible.

The aim here is to suggest that there is a class of religious beliefs— perhaps all of them, or all of the important ones—that are usually known to be true by their believers *immediately*. That is, they are known to be true by their believers without need to engage in reasoned analysis, assessment of evidence, or (emphatically) convincing others of their truth. It seems uncontroversial to assert that one does not need to be able to prove the truth of one's beliefs to someone who does not share them in order to know that they are true. I know that the claims *my tendency to arrogance is a direct product of my insecurity* and *I lost my virginity when I was fifteen years old* are true, though I might be hard pressed to demonstrate their truth to a doubter.

One problem with this kind of move is that it seems to make knowledge of the truth of what is expressed in the doctrine-expressing sentences of some religious community altogether too easy to come by. If the truth of *there is a Great Pumpkin who returns to the pumpkin patch every Hallowe'en to save our souls* is immediately evident to Pumpkinites and the truth of *none but God in Christ can save souls* is immediately evident to Christians, and the truth of *there are no souls to be saved* is immediately evident to Buddhists, then it would seem to follow from this that the Pumpkinite, the Christian, and the Buddhist have knowledge of the truth of claims whose truth-conditions and entailments make them incompatible one with another. And this cannot be right, for it is clear that two logically incompatible claims cannot both be true (and thus cannot both be known to be true). The only exit from this position is into some non-cognitivist reading of the doctrine-expressing sentences of religious communities, of one of the kinds already discussed and rejected in chapter 2.

This should suggest that the Pumpkinites have not in fact discharged all their epistemic duties by appealing to proper basicality or truth by immediate acquaintance. And this is why I chose to construct an imaginary example rather than to draw upon some actual one: the fact that the basic religious belief of the Pumpkinites is one that, on the face of it, seems unlikely to be shared by many outside the community, one that moreover seems very unlikely to gain acceptance by many reasonable people, is intended to suggest that the epistemic duties of the representative intellectuals of any religious community are controlled not only by the beliefs expressed through the doctrine-expressing sentences they enunciate and defend, but also by the broader sociocultural and religious context in which they find themselves.

To put this more simply: representative intellectuals of the Pumpkinite community must, if they are honest, acknowledge that rather few individuals share in their apparent immediate, direct, and unmediated access to knowledge of the truth of the central doctrine-expressing sentences of the Pumpkinite community. Further, they must acknowledge that there are other religious communities whose representative intellectuals claim with equal justification to have identical access to knowledge of the truth of their central doctrine-expressing sentences—and that these latter are, at least sometimes, directly incompatible with Pumpkinite doctrines. The epistemic duties of a community in this situation are not the same as those of a community in isolation, a community unaware of the religiously committed other.

The situation of the Pumpkinites leaves them only two options. The first is a retreat into fideism and its inevitable concomitant, sectarianism: an attempt to ignore the fact of religious pluralism, to build strong walls around the community, and so to prevent its members from becoming aware, in any detailed and existentially genuine sense, of the existence and nature of religious communities other than their own. The second is to acknowledge the facts, to realize that the epistemic duties of the community now require it to enter into both positive and negative apologetics, and to abandon the now untenable position that epistemic duty can be discharged without using positive apologetics. And, of course, all religious communities are now, more or less, in the situation of the Pumpkinites.

4.4 THE ARGUMENT THAT POSITIVE APOLOGETICS IS UNNECESSARY FOR THE PRESERVATION OF ETHICAL RESPECTABILITY

I shall now turn, with more brevity, to the objection that a community's ethical obligations can be fulfilled without ever turning to positive apologetics. There is, I think, one important situation in which the ethical imperative placed upon the representative intellectuals of a religious community to engage in positive apologetics is unavoidable; it has already been adverted to in chapter 1, and is a situation in which religious communities — especially those that fall under the umbrella of one of the "world religions" — very commonly find themselves.

If a particular religious community regards assent to a particular set of doctrine-expressing sentences as salvifically significant, and if it further thinks of the salvation of nonmembers as possessing some ethical significance, then it cannot, without considerable conceptual difficulty, avoid the conclusion that those who do not assent to the set of doctrine-expressing sentences in question should, for their own ultimate good, be brought to do so. For example: followers of Nichiren, a thirteenth-century Japanese Buddhist reformer, typically think that rebirth in the Pure Land can be attained only through faith in the *Lotus Sutra*, a sacred text of unparalleled importance in Nichiren's understanding of the Buddhist tradition, faith exhibited by chanting the *nam myoho renge kyo*, "homage to the *Lotus Sutra*." Since rebirth in the Pure Land is, by definition, the final salvific goal, and since all beings should ultimately attain it, the ethical imperative to bring it to the notice of all beings should be evident.

Recognition of this imperative will often carry with it an awareness that beings who do not acknowledge the importance of the *Lotus* should be shown the error of their belief-forming and belief-maintenance practices by the judicious application of positive apologetics. This will be especially relevant where the interlocutor is not just non- or antireligious, but has some prior and different religious conviction. This ethical imperative was certainly felt by Nichiren: he was perhaps the most accomplished (and vituperative) polemicist and apologist that Japan has ever produced. His apologetic was directed principally against those Buddhist sects whose doctrines he judged to be significantly opposed to his own views.

The ethical duty to engage in positive apologetics will thus very often take the form of an imperative, one of profound importance for a community's own self-understanding. It should be sufficiently obvious not to need further elaboration that the best, perhaps the only, way of meeting this ethical imperative in the circumstances described by the NOIA principle is to engage in positive apologetics.

4.5 THE ARGUMENT THAT POSITIVE APOLOGETICS IS IDOLATRY

The final objection to the necessity for engagement in positive apologetics comes usually from those religious communities that have an especially deep anti-intellectual stance (some examples of this were mentioned in chapter 1), or from those that place an especially high value on revelation as a source (perhaps, in extreme cases, even the only source) of necessary religious knowledge. For the latter type, typically, engagement in positive apologetics can easily be seen as a form of idolatry, an attempt to usurp a function proper to God by attributing to unaided human reason the ability to arrive at true judgements about the nature of things. Such an attitude, while it has been common in many theistic religious communities, leads to extremely undesirable consequences, among which I can mention only the more unpleasant.

For some Christian thinkers, especially those for whom John Calvin is a numinous figure, human beings are thought of as having a *sensus divinitatis*, a God-given faculty through which God's presence and activity in the world can be directly known. If (and perhaps only if) this faculty is operating as it should, knowledge of God and God's intentions is possible. Further, there is nothing that human beings can do to try and bring this faculty into operation; that too is God's will and God's doing. There is thus nothing that either can or should impel those whose God-given sense of God is in proper working order toward an exercise of their theological wits aimed at showing those who deny God's presence and activity that there is some problem with their cognitive habits and belief-forming mechanisms; much less that it is cognitively preferable to believe theistically than not to do so, and both negative and positive apologetics are thus rejected. The end result, for a religious community that holds such a view, is that the religious community comes to be viewed as a divinely appointed intellectual ghetto, whose boundaries, though very well defended, are almost impermeable. Entry into such a community (by having the right beliefs and engaging in the right practices) becomes a gift that God and God alone gives; human ingenuity, intellectual and otherwise, is irrelevant to it.

I referred to this as an unpleasant result of the view that engagement in positive apologetics is a species of idolatry. Its unpleasantness has two aspects: first, it creates (and here Calvin's own life is an excellent example) radical and pressing uncertainty. For it may seem to believers that their *sensus divinitatis* is working properly, but they can never be quite sure that it is, much less that it will continue to do so. Second (and this, perhaps, is the most damaging criticism of all) it may often make an ethical duty that the community on other grounds would hold itself to possess—such as the duty to aid the salvation of all human beings—impossible to fulfil. A theologian might say that fideism, and even perhaps antinomianism, would result. The position is not, of course, refuted by such observations; to do that would require entry into specific cases and an attempt to show: (1) either that a community that holds this view or something like it is thereby prevented from fulfilling some other duty that its doctrine-expressing sentences make incumbent upon it; (2) or that the view issues in some other markedly undesirable practical response—undesirable, that is, from the viewpoint of the community itself.

More need not, I think, be said about this argument against conceiving positive as, in certain circumstances, a duty. It has not, historically, been an objection of great importance in very many religious communities. I conclude that the arguments surveyed in this chapter provide no decisive reason for abandoning the recommendation to positive apologetics contained in the NOIA principle. It remains, in the next chapter, to draw together the threads of the argument thus far by setting forth briefly the conditions under which a proper apologetic must operate.

5

Proper Apologetics

In this chapter I shall state, as briefly as possible, the conditions that must obtain before a particular apologetical exercise can be judged proper. Most of these conditions have been mentioned in passing in the preceding chapters; here they will be brought together and their connections made clear. I shall consider first the political conditions that must be met before apologetics can properly be entered upon; then the expectations with which apologists should engage one another; and finally, the uses, if any, of self-guaranteeing community-specific authority sources within the apologetical enterprise.

5.1 THE POLITICAL CONTEXT

There is always a political context for an apologetical engagement. Just as intellects are never disembodied (at least in this world), so religious communities and their representative intellectuals are never without connections to the systems that structure and apply political, military, and economic power. Sometimes those connections will be explicit and overt, as in the case of Shi'ite Islam in contemporary Iran; sometimes they will be very visible but more symbolic than real, as in the case of the Anglican Church in England; sometimes they will be indirect but effective, as in the case of the Theravada Buddhist monastic order in Sri Lanka or the Moral Majority in the United States. But always, even in the case of the most self-consciously separatist and sectarian religious community (such as, for example, the Amish in the United States), there is a political context: the acts of the community, and especially its apologetical acts, will, because they must, have political effects. Every communal act is, more or less, an exercise of power, and this is especially true of positive apologetics; it is therefore especially important that aspiring apologists be self-conscious about this dimension of their actions.

I wish to argue that there are certain types of political situations that make the apologetical enterprise not only inadvisable but actually reprehensible. This may be true even when all the conditions envisaged by the NOIA principle obtain: sometimes, then, political considerations both may and should override the ethical and epistemic imperatives present in the NOIA principle.

Recall that, as I have outlined the enterprise in this book, apologetics is an occasional discipline, not a systematic one. That is to say, it is occasioned by a particular encounter, a particular realization on the part of the representative intellectuals of some religious community that the doctrine-expressing sentences to which they assent are challenged in an interesting way by those of some other religious community. It is not, or should not be, a systematic enterprise, an attempt in the privacy of the intellectual's study to show that the set of doctrine-expressing sentences to which one assents is in toto conceptually or epistemically superior to that of any possible competitor. Since positive apologetics is occasional in this sense, it is incumbent upon the apologist to be sensitive to the political dimensions of the occasion, and to be aware of the possibilities of exploitation and oppression inherent in it.

Consider the situation of a religious community closely linked to (or even identical with) the power structures of a dominant colonial nation. The Anglican Church perhaps held such a position during the expansionist days of the British Empire; the Buddhist monastic community may have held such a position at the time of Asoka in India; and it seems fairly clear that Islam was in just such a position as Abu Bakr entered Palestine in the early seventh century c.e. For a representative intellectual of a religious community in such a position to enter into positive apologetics vis-à-vis representatives of some religious community in the colonized and subordinate area is at best dangerous, and at worst ethically indefensible. This is because the reality of the situation will often be that the apologetic in question is an ex post facto justification of the military and economic dominance already in place, and so not a genuine apologetic at all. When apologetical arguments rest upon an assumption, explicit or implicit, of ethnic or cultural superiority, they are dangerous. They will not produce the benefits claimed for apologetics in this study, and will not be received by those at whom they are aimed as an apologetic, but rather as a thinly veiled — and sometimes quite open — application of military or economic pressure.

To generalize the points made here: there are several factors that, severally and conjointly, make positive apologetics improper. First, when positive apologetics is an integral part of a program of military, economic, or cultural imperialism, it is improper. Second, when engagement in positive apologetics is backed by the threat of violence against those at whom it is directed, it is improper. Third, where positive apologetics is based, in the minds of those who engage in it, upon an unshakable assumption of ethnic or cultural superiority, or upon a certainty that one's assent to the doctrine-expressing sentences for which one argues can never be altered, it is improper. I shall return to this third condition for impropriety in 5.2.

It might now be properly wondered whether there are many political situations in which positive apologetics can properly be engaged. It is probably the case that most instances of interreligious interaction in human history have taken place in situations where at least one of the conditions adverted to in the preceding paragraph was operative. But not all have. The extensive record of Hindu-Buddhist debate in India from the fourth to the eleventh centuries of the Christian era — much of which can properly be called positive apologetics — is, in large part, simply a vital component of the record of the religious and intellectual life of India, and not the record of the oppression of one group by another. Nichiren's vehement polemic against Shinran and Honen in thirteenth-century Japan is not noticeably marked by any of the conditions mentioned in the preceding paragraph. And even Peter the Venerable's apologetic against Islam in twelfth-century Europe, developed as it was at the time of the Crusades, is the work of a man who appears to have rejected the idea of the Crusades as a simple adventure in military conquest.

And in the modern period, it can be argued, political situations in which positive apologetics is a possibility are even more common. Preeminently, the academies of the West (perhaps especially in the USA) are institutions whose ideals are such that they make the perfect location for the development and application of a proper apologetic. And since these ideals are, to some extent at least, reflected in reality, there is no reason to rule out the university as the proper location for the polemical exercises in which positive apologetics consists. This is especially true when one remembers how many representative intellectuals of religious communities are sheltered by the academy in Europe, Japan, and the United States. More broadly still, the explicit links between religious communities and the exercise of political and military power in the modern world are fewer and more tenuous than they have been at most periods of human history. This is due in part to the fact that national identity increasingly provides what religious identity used to; it is due also to post-Enlightenment secularism. But whatever the long-term causes, it is surely beyond doubt that there are at least some sociopolitical contexts in which the application of interreligious apologetics is proper.

It may, of course, be argued that even the academy cannot be separated to the extent that I suggest from an oppressive nexus of power relations, and that any apologetical exercise undertaken within its walls is of necessity to be rejected because of this. It is certainly the case that, say, universities in the United States and in Western Europe are located in — and to some extent defined by — their often oppressive uses of power. But, as far as I can tell, such oppressive uses of power are principally classist, racist, and sexist rather than directed by one religious group against another. Indeed, the traditional connections between Christian churches and Western academies have been diluted to the extent that the boot, when there is one, is often on the other foot. A single example: in the state-run universities of the United States, funded as they are by state legislatures whose members consider themselves bound by a constitution whose first amendment forbids the making of any law establishing a particular religion, it is difficult to justify the expenditure of state funds on the teaching of Christianity by convinced and committed Christians—or at least by those who are publicly visible as such. It is therefore rare, and a potential cause for public controversy, to find a priest or minister teaching Christianity in such an institution. It is less rare, and apparently less a cause for controversy, to find a Buddhist monk teaching Buddhism in such an institution.

So, while the university is not value-free or free from oppressive uses of power and money, it is not the case that a proper apologetic is impossible in such a context. Neither, I think, is it the case that the possibility of oppression makes it always, or even often, impossible to rule out the undertaking of a proper apologetic by the representatives of particular religious communities in particular settings; I wish only to emphasize that the possibility of oppression should be present to the minds of such representatives when they begin their apologetical exercises.

5.2 THE EXPECTATIONS OF THE APOLOGIST

Apologists are people; apologetics is an activity; and people usually engage in activities with some expectations. In popular usage, perhaps, apologetics has come to be identified with any defensive argument in support of a predetermined orthodoxy: the expectation here is that of vindicating some position whose truth is already known on other, independent, grounds. Even if the meaning of the term is extended, as it has been in this study, to include positive apologetics, it might still be assumed that the expectation of the apologist is single and simple: victory. I wish to argue that although the expectations of the apologist may properly be for both vindication and victory, they should not be limited to these; further, I want to suggest that these are not the most important benefits to be gained from engagement in apologetics, and that a closer look at the reasons why this is so will shed a good deal of light upon the nature of a proper apologetic.

First, the expectation of vindication often and easily shades over into the simply vindictive; and the desire for victory in debate is hard to separate from the urge to grind one's opponents' faces into the dust. All debaters have felt the surge of adrenalin that accompanies the scoring of a point; and all academicians have felt the urge for vindication produced by the cutting phrases of reviewers who have, of course, completely misunderstood the nature of their work. These motivations and desires are felt even more strongly by religious apologists: if one is vindicating Buddha or winning a victory for YHWH over the heathen, the blood is likely to run even hotter than it does in defense of one's cherished theories or in the attempted conquest of one's intellectual enemies. These motivations and expectations are not necessarily ignoble, but, for some of the reasons explained in 5.1, they are dangerous. They can too easily lead to exploitation and oppression, to an exercise of one's wits for the sake of the exercise, and so to an unholy glee in the successful prosecution of another victory. And these expectations are most often apparent in political situations where proper apologetics is scarcely possible in any case.

A corrective is possible if the proponents of some particular positive apologetic are prepared to shape their expectations partly in terms of problem-solving and learning rather than solely in terms of vindication and victory. Vindication and victory may, of course, result; but if the apologist's eyes are always on them, many of the greatest benefits of entering into apologetics are likely to be missed. The expectations of proper apologists, then, will begin with skepticism as to the likelihood of all the doctrine-expressing sentences upon whose behalf they are engaging in apologetics being true. Such skepticism will take different forms depending upon the conceptual background of the religious community to which the apologist belongs. For many Christians it will include a realization that all human formulations that have to do with the central mysteries of the faith are very likely to be inadequate, subject to revision, and, on occasion, simply to be abandoned—and that all this may turn out to be true even of some one or more of the most cherished doctrine-expressing sentences of the community. For many Buddhists it will include a realization that, since all doctrine-expressing sentences are instrumental in producing Nirvana and none is descriptive of it, it may not be necessary to hold fast to any particular formulation, to any particular doctrine-expressing sentence, as uniquely productive of the desired transformation in its hearers or readers. Many other scenarios are possible. Such an expectation might allow the possibility of the apologetical enterprise resulting in the abandonment of one or more previously cherished doctrine-expressing sentences.

It is important to remember at this point that a passionate belief in, commitment to, and engagement with apologetics on behalf of some doctrine-expressing sentence does not necessarily bring with it—much less presuppose—certainty that one knows the doctrine-expressing sentence in question to be true. Faith, to put the matter in Christian terms, is not the same as either psychological certainty or justified true belief in regard to any doctrine-expressing sentence; much less, therefore, can it be the same as either psychological certainty in regard to the possession of such justified true belief, or knowledge that one has such justified true belief. While one may both know the truth of some doctrine-expressing sentence and know that one does, such a situation is rare in the extreme, and not required for engagement in positive or negative apologetics.

Proper apologists will engage in their enterprise with passion; with a powerful trust in the truth and efficacy of the doctrine-expressing sentences on whose behalf they enter the lists; but also with an awareness that engaging in the enterprise may lead them to abandon the same doctrine-express-ing sentences, or to modify them significantly.

It cannot be stressed too much that such an attitude need not in any way reduce the extent of the apologist's passion and commitment — both essential ingredients in the development of a powerful and proper apolo-getic. But a full and conscious appropriation of it will open the door to expectations that go beyond vindication and victory to learning and prob-lem-solving. As I shall attempt to illustrate with a case study in the final chapter, proper apologists will be self-conscious about the fact that there is no better tool for learning about the entailments and problems of the doctrine-expressing sentences to which they are committed than engage-ment in sincere and passionate apologetic on their behalf vis-à-vis one committed to some set of doctrine-expressing sentences that appears incompatible with their own. The expectation of learning and of problem-solving will thus be among the primary motivations and expectations of the proper apologist; they will go hand in hand with the ethical and epistemic obligations outlined in chapter 1, and given extended discussion in chapter 4. But it will often be the case that the most direct and obvious benefits of engagement in the apologetical enterprise will be heuristic, and will accrue to the constructor of the apologetic rather than to its recipient.

A final point on this: it is one of the advantages of including the expec-tations of learning and problem-solving among those with which proper apologists enter upon their task that one can, finally and with relief, dispose of the idea than one needs to be right in order to properly engage in interreligious apologetics. A good part of the benefits of the activity will accrue even if one turns out to be wrong, to have to revise or reject one of the doctrine-expressing sentences on whose behalf one engaged in the apol-ogetic in the first place. And this is, or can be, a liberating realization.

5.3 COMMUNITY-SPECIFIC, SELF-GUARANTEEING AUTHORITY SOURCES

This ground has already been covered in outline in chapter 1. Here, in the context of exploring the conditions governing proper apologetics, it simply needs to be reemphasized that appeals to community-specific self-guaranteeing authority sources can have no place therein. Such appeals, if made, will almost inevitably make it impossible for the benefits of a proper apologetic to be realized.

A community-specific self-guaranteeing authority source is any source taken by some specific religious community or some specific group of such to be productive of sentences that both express doctrines of the community and are true. It must also be a source whose deliverances require nothing other than their origin in the source in question to guarantee their status both as doctrine-expressing sentences of the community and as true sentences. The source may be a text, a person, or an experience had by some individual. I can think of no other possibilities.

There are many instances of texts being understood in just this way by religious communities. Paradigmatic, perhaps, is the orthodox Islamic view of the Qur'an: its deliverances possess authority for the community just because it is the uncreated word of God, delivered by the Archangel Gabriel to the prophet Muhammad and mediated through him to the scribes who recorded it unchanged for posterity. Some conservative Protestant Christians seem to have a very similar view of the King James or Authorized English version of the Old and New Testaments.

Some specific person can also act as a self-guaranteeing authority source for some religious communities. The Pope, in his ex cathedra utterances, is perhaps seen by some Roman Catholics as doing so. Any member of the class of fully awakened beings known as Buddhas—although these are perhaps "persons" only in a rather idiosyncratic sense of that term—functions in this way for many Buddhists. And so forth.

Finally, there may be some experiences had by some individual that act as a self-guaranteeing authority source for some religious communities. Experiential sources of this kind are a little difficult to distinguish from textual and personal ones, since all individual experiences are, because they must be, mediated to the community through texts or persons. But it is perhaps not impossible to distinguish an experiential self-guaranteeing authority source from a textual or personal one, and it may even be argued that both of the latter kinds are always rooted in the former. Textual self-guaranteeing authority sources are such, it may be argued, just because of the experiences that gave rise to them; and personal self-guaranteeing authority sources are such not simply in virtue of the status of the persons in question, but rather because of the experiences these persons have had.

Whatever the case may turn out to be—and the issue could be pursued with profit far beyond the brief sketch offered here—it should now be clear enough what is meant by a self-guaranteeing authority source. It should also be evident why appeals to such must be ruled out for the proper apologist. If such appeals are made as an integral part of an apologetical argument, the discussion cannot be properly joined and the benefits of apologetical argumentation will remain largely unrealized. This is because the very fact that the authority source in question is community-specific means that it is accepted as an authority source by only one side in the debate, and can therefore cut no apologetical ice. The Islamic apologist who appeals to the Qur'an to justify all his arguments for the cognitive superiority of Islamic theism over and against some version of Buddhist transpolytheism will not get very far; neither will the Buddhist who attempts the same job in reverse by quoting the *Lotus Sutra*. This is not to say that self-guaranteeing authority sources have no place in the belief-forming and belief-maintenance habits of properly regulated religious communities. On the contrary: they both do and must. Rather few religious communities can manage without them, and it is perfectly conceivable that some one or more than one of those sources of doctrine-expressing sentences regarded as both authoritative and self-guaranteeing by some religious community might actually be what the representative intellectuals of that community judge it to be. But it is to affirm that no appeal to them considered as such can properly be made by a representative intellectual of any religious community when engaged in apologetics.

It might be suggested at this point that my ban on the use of community-specific self-guaranteeing authority sources is improper because it demands of religious communities that think of themselves as possessing such a source that they pretend, inauthentically, not to have such a source when they engage in apologetics. However, the requirement here is not that such religious communities abandon tout court a conviction that is integral to their own self-understanding; that would certainly be inauthentic. I am suggesting instead that, on straightforwardly practical grounds, such sources should not be used *as self-guaranteeing authority sources* in an apologetical debate. An apologetical argument may, of course, be mounted in support of regarding the source in question as authoritative; but such an argument should not presuppose that the source is authoritative. The circularity in such an argument would be vicious; and such an argument would be useless.

A final point here: self-guaranteeing authority sources do have a place in interreligious apologetics, but only when one or both of the following conditions is met. Either the authority source in question must be recognized as such by both sides in the debate — as when Christians and Jews debate the meaning of passages in the Hebrew Bible acknowledged as authoritative by both sides. Or, apologetical arguments independent of the authority source in question must be provided for its status as such — as when Christians try to convince Jews of the status of the New Testament as authority source by appealing to its fulfillment of certain passages in the Hebrew Bible already regarded as authoritative by the Jews.

6

Apologetics in Action: Buddhists and Christians on Selves

What are human persons? How are they constituted? What are their essential properties and proper goals? These are issues of concern to all religious communities. What a particular community judges a person to be has direct effects upon, and is itself affected by, what that community thinks about the ethical codes governing the lives of those within the community, and about such purely metaphysical questions as the nature of continuing identity through time. The representative intellectuals of religious communities have therefore typically devoted a good deal of time and attention to discussing what is and what is not an acceptable view of the person. This is an issue with great potential for the apologist since, as I shall try to show, representative intellectuals of different religious communities have sometimes developed radically different views about it, views that they perceive as being determinative for everything that is of value to the community. A classic case of such difference is brought to light by contrasting the standard-issue Buddhist position on the nature of the person with the standard-issue Christian position on the same question; and this is what I shall attempt in the remainder of this chapter.

There is no such thing as *the* Buddhist or *the* Christian position on this matter — or on any other. Both Buddhism and Christianity are far too complex, internally differentiated, and subtle for anything so straightforward. Instead, there have been and are many philosophico-theological positions on the nature of the human person adhered to and argued for by Christian intellectuals. Some of these are significantly different from others, some so different as to create the necessity for intra-Christian apologetics among different Christian religious communities. So also for Buddhism: the position argued for by, say, the fourth-century Indian scholastic Vasubandhu in his work on the subject entitled *Negation of the Person*, is significantly different from that implicit in the thirteenth-century Japanese thinker Dogen's *Shobogenzo.*

In speaking, as I shall in what follows, of *a* Buddhist and *a* Christian position on the nature of the person, I do not intend to suggest that all Buddhists or all Christians would even recognize the positions I shall outline, much less assent to them. I want only to sketch positions that represent some of the more important trajectories of thought and intellectual strategies visible in the works of the representative intellectuals of each tradition, and so to create an artificial construct, at a high level of generality, that is likely to reflect precisely no single specific Buddhist's or Christian's position on the matter under discussion. My purposes in creating such a construct are heuristic: I hope to show, by dealing with a specific issue in a certain amount of detail, that the benefits claimed in earlier chapters for engagement in apologetics are not entirely illusory.

6.1 A BUDDHIST REJECTION OF THE SELF

Buddhist metaphysics is generally reductionist in its goals and analytical in its methods. It is interested not in those medium-sized pieces of dry goods that the naive intellect takes to really exist, but rather in their component parts. It hopes, by an analytical deconstruction of what appears to be solid and enduring, to remove deceptive belief-forming habits and to make it possible to arrive at an apprehension of those irreducible basic existents that are the constituents of everything other than themselves; or, alternatively, to come to a clear realization of the fact that there are no such basic existents, and that every attempt on the part of human beings to individuate existents, to mark them off one from another, will necessarily fail. Those Buddhist metaphysicians who took the former route labeled their irreducible basic existents "dharmas" and called themselves "abhidharmikas" — than which there is no better translation than "metaphysician." Those who took the latter route called themselves "shunyavadins" or "advocates of emptiness."

Debates between the metaphysicians and the advocates of emptiness fill the folios of the doxographical and polemical compendia produced by Buddhist intellectuals in India and Tibet. And each debate spawned in its turn subdebates and subschools, dividing metaphysician against metaphysician and advocate of emptiness against advocate of emptiness. But for my purposes the details of these intra-Buddhist disputes need not be pursued, since the method of analytical deconstruction is common to both sides in the debate (and, indeed, is shared by other groups not mentioned here), and the effects of this method on Buddhist views of the person are what matters for this study.

According to many non-Buddhist Indian philosophico-religious schools, to be a human person is precisely to be a spiritual substance (variously called *atman, jiva,* or *purusha*) connected temporarily with a psychophysical organism. One way of thinking of this relation is that the spiritual substance — that in virtue of which a given human person is who he or she is and not someone else — possesses the psychophysical organism as one of its contingent attributes, one of its "accidents" as medieval Western scholastics would have put it. As the *Bhagavadgita* says, the Self takes on and puts off bodies during the course of its existence just as a man takes on and puts off suits of clothes during the course of a single embodied existence. The uppercase "S" here is meant to indicate that this is not the phenomenal, changing self that is the subject of ordinary temporal experience, and that is constituted by the ordinary person's sense of one's own identity, but rather the unchanging metaphysical subject that, in some sense, acts as the locus or support for all such experience and all such sense of identity — the Sanskrit term is *atman.* My clothes, on this view, are not essential properties of me. The fact that I possess the property *wearing blue jeans on 12 February 1989* says nothing about my essential nature, supposing that I have one, and certainly does not individuate me uniquely. There may be many other human persons with an identical property. The *Bhagavadgita* seems to suggest something similar about the relation between Selves and bodies.

The important point about this example from a non-Buddhist Indian tradition is that it illustrates graphically that which the Buddhist analytical deconstruction is concerned to reject. Buddhist intellectuals wanted to rebut the idea that there is an enduring spiritual substance, something analogous to (though not identical with) what Christians have meant by the term "soul," which gives to individual human beings their true identity. This, from the Buddhist standpoint, is a fundamental and damaging conceptual error, and Buddhists devoted an enormous amount of intellectual energy to demonstrating, or trying to demonstrate, that such a view is ill-founded, and to offering a rival and radically antisubstantivist view in its place. I shall offer some comments on the arguments offered against a substantivist view below; for the moment I shall concentrate upon an exposition of the nonsubstantivist view of human persons defended by Buddhist metaphysicians, and of the method of analytical reduction used to arrive at it.

Consider the example of a chariot, often used by Buddhist metaphysicians in India as an analogue for the Self. The following passage presents a discussion between Nagasena, a Buddhist monk, and King Milinda, an Indian monarch needing instruction in basic Buddhism:

[Nagasena addresses Milinda]:
"Now, did you come on foot or in a conveyance?"
"I, revered sir, did not come on foot, I came in a chariot."
"If you, sire, came by chariot, show me the chariot. Is the pole the chariot, sire?"
"O no, revered sir."
"Is the axle the chariot?"

"O no, revered sir."

"Are the wheels the chariot?"

"O no, revered sir."

"Is the body of the chariot the chariot . . . is the flag-staff of the chariot
the chariot . . . is the yoke the chariot . . . are the reins the chariot
. . . is the goad the chariot?"

"O no, revered sir."

"But then, sire, is the chariot the pole, the axle, the wheels, the body
of the chariot, the flag-staff of the chariot, the yoke, the reins, the
goad?"

"O no, revered sir."

"But then, sire, is there a chariot apart from the pole, the axle, the
wheels, the body of the chariot, the flag-staff of the chariot, the
yoke, the reins, the goad?"

"O no, revered sir."

"Though I, sire, am asking you repeatedly, I do not see the chariot.
Chariot is only a sound, sire. For what here is the chariot? You,
sire, are speaking an untruth, a lying word. There is no chariot."

A chariot is a composite thing. Nagasena asks Milinda whether any one
of its parts can be identified with what the word "chariot" refers to. The
answer, as expected, is that no specific part can be so identified: a BMW,
to update the example, is not its wheels, its engine, its leather seats, or its
chassis. Nagasena then asks whether it is the case that the chariot is all of
its parts together, and once again the answer is no. The word "BMW" does
not refer simply to the totality of all the parts that are present in any
particular automobile of that type.

The third option given to Milinda by Nagasena is to say that the word
"chariot" refers to something other than the parts of which a chariot is
comprised, and here too the answer is negative: there is no existent other
than the axle, wheels, and so forth, to which it is proper to say that the
term "chariot" refers. The conclusion is straightforward: "I do not see the
chariot. Chariot is only a sound . . . There is no chariot."

The question at issue here is whether certain kinds of words refer to
anything. Human beings commonly use words that, in unreflective moments,
they take to refer to or label medium-sized pieces of dry goods. "Chariot"
is one such word. "BMW" is another. Simply because such things as chariots
and BMWs are medium-sized pieces of dry goods, they are necessarily
composite: they are extended in space, have parts, and can, theoretically
and usually practically, be physically divided into those parts. One can
dismember a chariot, if one is so inclined, though doing so will tend to
destroy its usefulness as a chariot.

The position taken in the short extract just discussed is that anything
composite, anything with parts, does not really exist just because there are
more basic constituents that make it up. Words that appear to refer to or

label composite things therefore cannot really do so, because the kind of existence such things have is a purely conventional one: in the absence of the needs and desires of the person or group undertaking the labeling, there is nothing present to label.

This is not to say that words such as "chariot" should not be used. Given the communicative and practical needs and goals of groups of human beings, such words are indispensable. The mistake lies not in using such words but in thinking that they reflect or label items among the furniture of the universe. It is perfectly reasonable to speak of BMWs and Chevrolets, just so long as speakers are aware in so doing that they speak with and for the vulgar and not with and for the philosophically sophisticated. Such discourse is instrumental: it labels and denotes nothing.

Given such an analytical and reductionist method, two ontologies are possible. The first, that of the Buddhist metaphysician, states that there are basic irreducible existents, partless constituents of all medium-sized pieces of dry goods, and that these can be arrived at precisely by the application of the analytical reduction. Certain kinds of language, on this view, are capable of reference and denotation: it is possible to speak about the irreducible indivisible existents that comprise the cosmos in a noninstrumental way. The second ontology, that of the Buddhist advocate of emptiness, states that there are no such constituents; that all attempts to individuate existents one from another, to say "this is other than that," are entirely conventional, without reference to any existent things. On this ontology, reference or denotation is impossible and the analytical deconstruction has no end.

Whichever view is taken, whichever ontology is affirmed, chariots do not ultimately exist: and precisely the same is true of Selves. The analytical reduction is applied to the person in just the same way as to physical objects. In the case of the person, that entity observable by others as a physical body occupying space and enduring through time and experienceable to itself as a complex and continuing field of consciousness, the analytical reduction issues in a descriptive analysis of the person as consisting in five "heaps," "groups," or "aggregates" (*skandha*) of causally connected momentary events. And, just as with the chariot, the Self is said not to be identical with any one of these five "aggregates," nor with all of them together. Since, further, no other existent is perceptible when the analytical reduction is performed upon some particular person, it follows that there is no Self. And this is the fundamental Buddhist insight usually called the no-Self doctrine.

6.2 A BUDDHIST DESCRIPTION OF THE PERSON

To deny that there are Selves does not entail denying that there are persons, much less that personal proper names can, in certain contexts and with certain needs in view, properly be used. When such a name is used, though, it cannot be taken to refer to an enduring substance, but only as a description of a stream of momentary events bound together by causal connections of various kinds. The personal proper name "Nagarjuna" (to take an example from the history of Buddhist philosophy) describes, on this view, a stream of events of five kinds, corresponding to the five "aggregates" or "heaps" referred to at the end of the preceding section. Such a stream of events can be individuated from other such streams—say, that called "Vasubandhu" or that called "Asanga"—only conventionally: there is, on most Buddhist views, no rigid principle of individuation by which one "person" (in the Buddhist sense of that term) can be individuated from another, and the absence of such a principle occasioned many intra- and extra-Buddhist debates, as well as some attempts to construct one. None of these met with anything approaching universal assent among Buddhist intellectuals.

Something more should be said about the five aggregates or streams of events into which standard Buddhist analysis divides the person. A brief description of these will provide some insight into how persons were and are understood by Buddhist theoreticians. The first aggregate is that of physical form: it comprises all nonmental events belonging to a given person. The aggregate of physical form (*rupaskandha*) is all those causally connected physical events that comprise my body. It embraces those events whose presence gives both me and observers other than myself the impression that I possess (or, on a physicalist reading, simply am) a three-dimensional physical entity enduring through time.

Again, there are many intra-Buddhist debates about the exact nature and proper definition of physical form; these are beyond the scope of this study. All that matters for my purposes is to note that while the existence of some causally connected events of physical form is normal for human persons existing in this world-realm, such events are not required for the continued existence of the (conventionally speaking) "same" person. That persons can exist without any physical form at all, in a disembodied fashion, is evident from the many references to and descriptions of existence in cosmic realms wherein there is no physical form of any kind. The possession of a body is therefore not constitutive of any human person on the usual Buddhist view.

The second aggregate is that of sensation (*vedana-skandha*). This comprises all types of affect, all positively or negatively toned responses to stimuli. Feeling pleased by a compliment is an instance of sensation-that-consists-in-pleasure (*sukhavedana*) as a Buddhist scholastic would put it, just as feeling pained by an insult is an example of sensation-that-consists-in-pain (*duhkhavedana*). All human persons include a stream of such causally connected affective events as part of the broader stream of events in which they consist. These events, like those of physical form classified under the first aggregate, are momentary and changeable. None lasts for more than a moment, and the very impermanence and unreliability of these moments of sensation is part of what the radical unsatisfactoriness (*duhkha*) of human life consists in for a Buddhist thinker.

The third aggregate is that of conceptualization (*samjñaskandha*). The momentary events included here are free of affect; instead, they apprehend and classify the defining characteristics of a particular moment of sensory experience, labeling each moment as an experience *of* something. As Vasubandhu, a fourth-century C.E. Buddhist scholastic put it: "The aggregate of conceptualization is the apprehension of the defining characteristics of things, for example [noting that some particular experience is an experience of] blue, yellow, long, short, woman, man, friend, enemy, pleasure, pain, and so forth." It is through the workings of the aggregate of conceptualization that all human persons construct for themselves a liveable world, since through the events that comprise this aggregate, persons develop and apply categories that make sense of experience and thus provide at least the illusion of a world containing continuing and predictable existents. The categories that any given human person makes use of in exercising one's aggregate of conceptualization will naturally be largely dependent upon the process of acculturation that has produced the person, and upon the person's needs and goals. A Buddhist would add that they are also dependent upon one's karmic condition, the karmic inheritance that one brings with one from previous lives.

The fourth aggregate is that of volitions (*samskara-skandha*). Where the second aggregate dealt with the realm of affect and the third with that of concept and the application of linguistic labels to phenomena, the fourth deals with the will, with conation. Given standard Buddhist presuppositions about the nature of action and its effects upon an agent, this means that the momentary events contained in any person's aggregate of volitions are, more than anything else, what govern that individual's future lives and what carry the effects of actions from past lives to the present. Karma simply is, in Buddhist terms, volitional action and its results. Buddhism, in its classical forms, is very far from determinism, and the standard Buddhist theory of the person clearly recognizes that an important part of any person is the free decisions one makes. Naturally, a libertarian or quasilibertarian view of persons and their choices does not entail or even suggest that there is an enduring agent making those choices. It would be more accurate to say that volitions are a species of mental event phenomenologically distinguishable from other mental events and not fully determined by those events that are their causal predecessors.

Fifth, and last, there is the aggregate of consciousness (*vijñanaskandha*), a term perhaps equally capable of translation as "cognition." An instance of consciousness or cognition occurs when one apprehends some object. One will typically do this through one or more of the sense organs, and so the standard Buddhist analysis of cognition divides it into six types depending upon which sense organ gave rise to it. Cognition may thus be mental, olfactory, gustatory, auditory, visual, or tactile. Notice the inclusion of mental cognition; this is a direct result of the standard Buddhist view that the mind (*manas*) is a sense organ in a manner precisely analogous to that in which the eye or the ear is. Cognition is always intentional: it has some object other than itself, and so is not self-reflexive. Cognition is also always prior to both the affective reactions comprised under the second aggregate, and to the classificatory activity comprised under the third. As Yashomitra, an eighth-century Indian Buddhist scholastic put it, when one apprehends an object through cognition one apprehends a bare undifferentiated object. One does not yet react affectively to it or classify it as something or other. It is simply present to one's awareness.

The streams of events included within these five aggregates are all that there is: any personal proper name refers to these and to these alone. There is nothing that underlies them or possesses them, no agent or thinker other than actions or thoughts, and certainly no enduring substance of which these aggregates are accidental and changing attributes. The analysis of the person into five streams of events is, in Buddhist eyes, an exhaustive analysis.

The production of such an analysis was not an analytical game for those who devoted so much intellectual energy to it; neither is it an analytical game for those Buddhists who continue to hold to this view of the human person. The motivation for developing and refining such a counterintuitive picture of what it is to be a human person — especially counterintuitive when one recalls that it was combined by Buddhist intellectuals with the pan-Asian view that every person has had many lives in the past and will have many more in the future — was soteriological; and it remains to explain the soteriological functions of the doctrine of no-Self.

The standard Buddhist analysis of the human condition follows, with self-conscious precision, the form of an ancient Indian medical diagnosis. First there is a description of the disease; then a statement of the disease's etiology; then a suggestion as to a probable cure; and finally a recommendation about therapy, the best course of action to engage in in order that the desired cure will be brought about. The disease is one of radical unsatisfactoriness: *duhkha*. Human life is marked by an endless cycle of birth, growth, decline, death, rebirth, redeath ... and so on. Every stage of this cyclical process is radically unsatisfactory in different ways and so involves different kinds of suffering. When one is born, one is helpless, powerless, and filled with fear of the unknown and desire for food. As one matures one becomes oppressed by sexual desires, by desires for fame, wealth, and power, and by conflicts with others. As one declines, one's body becomes a burden, one's mind fails, and one usually dies in agony. And the whole process repeats itself endlessly unless and until one can see how to destroy the motive forces that drive it. These motive forces are described when the disease's etiology is set forth. The principal among them is desire of all kinds (*trishna*), craving for goals. Closely associated with this is ignorance: a misapprehension as to which goals are properly desirable and, usually, a complete misunderstanding of the true nature of human persons and the things they crave. The cure is to uproot and destroy desire and its concomitant ignorance: when the cause of suffering is removed, suffering itself will vanish and human life will cease to be marked by radical unsatisfactoriness. And the therapy, the means to destroy desire and ignorance, is set forth in a detailed soteriological path (*marga*), beginning with proper ethical practice and culminating in a direct insight into the nature of things.

Perhaps the most important single factor from a Buddhist viewpoint contributing to the radical unsatisfactoriness of the human condition is the tendency human persons have to think that they are themselves centers of continuing identity and importance, to judge that there is some enduring entity referred to by their own proper name. Following directly from this tendency is the proclivity to judge that other human persons are similar: that other persons too are enduring entities with, perhaps, an eternal soul as that which really defines them. A view such as this is a variant on the heresy (from the Buddhist point of view) of "eternalism" (*shashvatavada*). It is consistently and vehemently opposed by Buddhist theoreticians. The reason should be clear: if passion, desire, and ignorance are the fundamental problems for human beings, and if, as seems evident, the most basic human passions are connected with the view that one's own needs should be fulfilled and that at least some other human beings are, or may be, worthy objects of attachment and desire, it will then follow that any view that contributes to the occurrence and maintenance of these passions should be removed. If one thinks that one is an enduring entity, one is likely to be concerned about one's future. If one thinks that others are enduring entities one is more likely to become attached to them—whether as lovers, friends, spouses, or offspring—than is the case if one judges them to consist only in causally connected streams of momentary events.

The Buddhist rejection of the Self, set forth briefly in 6.1, is thus intended primarily as a corrective to the occurrence of passion based upon a false view of the nature of the human person. A proper understanding of the Buddhist no-Self doctrine is an integral part of the Buddhist soteriological path: its truth is presupposed by those committed to the practice of that path, and unless it is true, that path has little coherence.

The very brief sketch given in this and the preceding section of a Buddhist position on the Self and the person suggests that at least the following doctrine-expressing sentences would be affirmed by representative intellectuals of Buddhist communities (though recall again my warnings about assuming that all Buddhist communities would assent to—or even recognize—the position set forth here): (1) *All personal proper names refer to causally-connected continua of events and to nothing else.* (2) *Intellectual understanding and personal appropriation of the truth of (1) is a necessary condition for the attainment of Nirvana.* (3) *Assent to any doctrine-expressing sentence contradicting (1) or any entailment thereof will necessarily be productive of suffering.* With these doctrine-expressing sentences in mind, I turn now to an exposition, equally brief and equally superficial, of a possible Christian position on the nature of the human person. I shall return to these sentences and to their Christian counterparts at the end of this chapter.

6.3 A CHRISTIAN DESCRIPTION OF THE PERSON AS EMBODIED SOUL

The representative intellectuals of most Christian religious communities have felt called upon to affirm that human persons do possess permanent souls; they have often also claimed that the identity of any particular human person consists precisely in the possession of the particular soul that one in fact possesses. Just as was the case with Buddhists, Christians do not make such claims for purely philosophical reasons (which is not to say that there are no philosophical reasons for them): interest in the soul and its nature is connected in intricate and complex ways with the views about salvation developed by the tradition, and, especially, with views about God's nature and purposes. Much of traditional Christian metaphysics and soteriology cannot stand if the Buddhist account of what constitutes a human person should turn out to be correct.

It is a fundamental doctrine of the Christian churches that all human persons are created by a transcendent, eternal, divine being, and that each human person reflects, in some manner and to some extent, the image or likeness of that divine being of whom one is a creation. This idea is rooted in the texts that are, for most Christian communities, possessed of sacred and divine authority. The Book of Genesis, for example, says:

> Then God said: "Let us make man in our image and likeness to rule the fish in the sea, the birds of heaven, the cattle, all wild animals on earth, and all reptiles that crawl upon the earth." [1:26]

Because of this revelational data, most Christian communities have made their doctrines about what human persons are more or less dependent upon their doctrines about what God is. Naturally, no human person is identical with God, so no human person will share all the attributes of the divinity. But since each and every human person is made in the "image and likeness" of God, it will follow that human persons must have some attributes in common with God: there must be some meaningful sense in which they are like God.

According to the doctrine-expressing sentences of most Christian communities, God has no body. God's incorporeality was understood, from the second century of the Christian era onward, to mean that God is a spiritual substance—that is, a nonmaterial entity possessed of attributes, enduring through time (or perhaps altogether transtemporal), and yet capable of entering into various causal relationships with material things. Human persons must reflect or image important elements of the divine attribute, so they too came to be regarded as essentially incorporeal. No human persons are identical with their bodies, because, among many other things, if they were, they would not be an image and likeness of their creator. Human persons then have the identity they have in virtue of the spiritual substance — the soul — that gives it to them.

In addition to the argument from likeness to the creator, there is an equally powerful argument from soteriological theory. The death of the body is not the death of the person. The hope of Christians is for eternal life: each person's proper destiny is to maintain a perfectly loving relationship with God for eternity. Given the obvious fact that such a relationship cannot be maintained in the body, for the body dies, it must be maintained incorporeally. And that which maintains it is a substance, which is the soul. Important here is the notion of continuity of identity. There is some important sense, as yet unspecified, in which a spiritual substance that enjoys eternal life in the presence of God must be continuous in identity with an embodied spiritual substance that prayed for such eternal life in church each Sunday before it ceased to be embodied. If this is not the case then it also cannot meaningfully be said that any Christians hope for salvation — or, indeed, for the salvation of any specific dead person. As the catechism contained in the Anglican *Book of Common Prayer* puts it:

Q: Why do we pray for the dead?
A: We pray for them, because we still hold them in our love, and because we trust that in God's presence those who have chosen to serve him will grow in his love, until they see him as he is.

Implied here, evidently, is the idea that persons do not cease with death; that they continue eternally beyond death; and that it makes sense for those persons now embodied to offer prayers for those no longer embodied. That which individuates one disembodied person from another and makes it proper to speak of some now disembodied person as continuous in identity with some previously embodied person, is the soul. Indeed, on some readings of Christian doctrine, disembodied persons consist only in souls — at least until the resurrection of the body, whatever is meant precisely by the rather puzzling set of doctrine-expressing sentences surrounding that particular affirmation.

So far I have suggested that Christian beliefs about enduring spiritual substances — especially beliefs about these substances as those things that make persons who they are — are motivated in part by the idea that human persons must resemble God in some significant fashion, and in part by the fact that beliefs about the final destiny of human persons seem to require that there be some nonphysical individuating principle of identity possessed by human persons.

But there is also, I think, a third motivation underlying traditional Christian affirmations about the soul, and this is historical rather than systematic. From the second century of the Christian era, at latest, Christian intellectuals were heavily influenced by the concepts, terminology, and philosophical agendas of non-Christian Hellenistic thinkers. And for these thinkers, ever since Plato and Aristotle (though the ideas of these two on the matter were quite different), the idea that human persons possess (or consist in) an immaterial substance (for which the Greek term *psuche* was often used) was central. Such an idea was often used by these philosophers as an *explanans*, a way of accounting for the perceived unity of the thinking and willing subject. If it is asked what provides the continuity perceptible in the ordinary experience of human persons between one moment of their experience and later moments—the sense that the same person, the same center of will and thought, is experiencing now as was experiencing earlier—the answer will tend to be given in terms of the continued existence of the soul, with its powers, in both moments. So, for example, Aristotle appeals to the soul in his discussion of memory: "For whenever someone is actively engaged in remembering, he always says in his soul in this way that he heard, or perceived, or thought this before." This sort of appeal to the soul as a necessary explanation for the experienced continuity of the human person as a center of will, memory, and thought, became a standard part of the intellectual equipment of most Christian thinkers.

In spite of these strong motives for affirming that the soul exists in something like the sense suggested, the representative intellectuals of Christian communities have not been so eager to give it precise definition. Those who have attempted to provide such a definition have usually later had it rejected as heretical. The Roman Catholic Church, when making pronouncements on the nature of the soul, has usually contented itself with rejecting whatever positions its representative intellectuals currently thought heretical, and has not gone very far in giving details as to how the soul should be understood. So, for example, the eternal preexistence of the soul with God was rejected at the Council of Constantinople in the sixth century; the idea that the soul is not in and of itself the governing and controlling principle of embodied human life was censured at the General Council of Vienna in 1311–12; and the idea that the soul is begotten by its possessor's parents was rejected by Benedict XII in 1341, as part of his condemnation of traducianism. The documents promulgated by the Roman Catholic Church at the Second Vatican Council in the 1960s scarcely mention the soul at all, and nowhere give it systematic treatment. The soul is given nothing but passing treatment in the 39 articles of the Anglican Church—and both the documents of Vatican II and the 39 articles are entirely typical of official church documents from all communions in this respect.

There are, of course, many detailed philosophico-theological treatments of the soul's essential nature by representative intellectuals of Christian communities from many times and places. But an exploration of these would tend to make this investigation more specific than I intend it to be. It will suffice for my purposes to say that insofar as the representative intellectuals of Christian communities have formulated doctrine-expressing sentences about souls, such sentences almost always affirm that the soul is immortal and so that its identity endures through time; that it was created at a particular time by God; that it is the bearer of moral responsibility, and so also (usually) the agent of morally qualified acts; that it is non-physical; and that in it is located a human person's volitional and intellectual life, as well as character. The soul is the structured seat of consciousness, the possessor of a complex and interrelated web of beliefs, intentions, habit-patterns, tendencies, and so forth.

Will it then suffice to say that any human person simply is the soul? This will not quite do because "person," too, is a technical term in Christian theology. The doctrine of the trinity was formulated in terms of three divine persons (*persona* in Latin, *hypostasis* or *prosopon* in Greek) sharing a single substance (*substantia* in Latin, *ousia* in Greek). In trinitarian theology, "person" is both a relational and an active term: the three divine persons are mutually related and mutually active, and it makes sense to speak of them as distinct persons only in terms of distinctions among the activities they undertake. The same emphasis on relationality and activity is evident in most Christian talk about human persons. Human persons are essentially relational in the sense that they exist fully only in a proper relationship with their creator; they are relational also in that they both do and should partially fulfil their proper ends in virtue of their relations with other human persons.

Clearly, then, to be an embodied human person in Christian terms is not simply to be the possessor of an immortal soul (though it is at least that). Being an embodied soul rather than a disembodied one makes possible the peculiar kind of relationality that characterizes human interpersonal relations. And it may also be that the possibilities for self-sacrificing love inherent in the embodied condition are such as to make some experience of it necessary if the soul's proper relation to God is ever to be realized. This, I think, is why many of the fathers of the church (especially in the Eastern churches) thought of embodied human persons, consisting of both the material and the spiritual, of both body and soul, as having greater complexity and greater potentiality than the purely spiritual (and so theoretically "higher") angels.

The importance of being embodied and the possibilities inherent in it are also shown, more clearly than in any other way, by the doctrine of the incarnation: the second person of the trinity, the incorporeal logos, becomes embodied for soteriological reasons. All this suggests that it is better to reserve the use of the term "person" in human contexts for embodied humans: to be a human person, because of the relationality and mutuality involved with such a condition, requires embodiment. Nevertheless, because the structured soul bears the essential properties of an embodied human person and can continue to bear them after the death of the body, it will still make sense to speak of "the same person" continuing to exist without one's body after death. The person's relationality then will be principally with God, and perhaps also with other disembodied human souls (though the representative intellectuals of Christian communities sensibly exhibit a good deal of agnosticism about the modalities of potential relationships among communities of disembodied human souls).

Given this kind of view of what an embodied person is, the representative intellectuals of Christian communities must necessarily give some account of how the soul—which, recall, is nonphysical, a spiritual substance—is related to the body, which is neither of these things. This is the question, to put it rather differently, of how the complex physicospiritual unity of the embodied human person is constituted. There are a number of logical possibilities here, but only one which has seriously claimed the attention of Christian intellectuals. In what follows I shall offer brief comments upon two views of the relationship between soul and body (or, more precisely, between soul and brain, since the brain is the physical object that must be most closely connected, causally, with the soul if the latter exists at all). I shall not be concerned with the systematic advantages and disadvantages of these positions—with whether they are likely to be true or not—but only with the ways in which they tend to be perceived and used by the representative intellectuals of Christian communities.

The first view is usually called epiphenomenalism; it claims that the mental events in which the soul consists are by-products of physical events. The most common version of this view says that all mental events are supervenient upon brain states: thus the possession of a (physical) brain is a necessary condition for the occurrence of any mental event, and thus for any of the activities of the soul. If this view is correct, one needs to be embodied in order to have a soul, for the possession of a soul is causally dependent upon the possession of a brain (and, presumably, upon that brain achieving a certain level of complexity and organization in its synaptic structure). The causal relations between brain and soul are entirely one-way. Epiphenomenalism is not simple materialism: it does allow that consciousness—the possession of a soul in Christian terms—is not identical with physical events. Brain states are not all that there is. But epiphenomenalism does make the soul entirely dependent for its existence upon the condition of being embodied, and this, naturally, rules out the possibility of the soul's disembodied existence.

This entailment of epiphenomenalism is sufficient to rule it out as a possible reading of the relations between soul and body for most Christian intellectuals. Though perhaps it should be noted that the view of the embodied person's nature found in some of the sacred texts of the tradition, especially those of the Hebrew Bible, can be interpreted in a way consonant with epiphenomenalism. The view is thus not entirely without supporters in Christian communities.

The second broad range of positions on the soul's relationship to the brain is more radically dualistic, and allows for two-way causal interactions. On this view, the soul is, as I have already suggested, a structured, enduring, nonphysical substance, consisting of beliefs, desires, intentions, dispositions, and so forth. It interacts causally with the brain, producing brain states (and the physical actions that follow from them) that accord with its structure. It, in its turn, is influenced causally by brain states that are produced by stimuli external to the soul: inputs from sensory interactions with other persons, from sensory interactions with the material world, and from interactions of various kinds with God or with other spiritual beings (angels, demons, and so forth). On this interactionist view, the soul is both shaped by its embodiedness and, in its turn, shapes the actions of the embodied person to whom it gives identity. This kind of dualistic analysis of the constitution of embodied persons has proved the most attractive option for the representative intellectuals of Christian communities, because it appears to meet the communities' needs in ways that no other view can. Dualist interactionism provides a theoretical position that will account for: the hope of the resurrection; the concomitant possibility of disembodied existence; the location of moral responsibility in an agent who can continue to exist after physical death; and the likeness of human persons to the eternal spiritual substance who is their creator.

In conclusion: the sketch given here of the Christian view of persons as embodied souls with the capacity to continue in existence after the death of the body as disembodied souls should require assent to at least the following doctrine-expressing sentences: (1) *The possession of an immortal soul gives every human person identity.* (2) *The immortal soul is an enduring spiritual substance with a temporal beginning but no temporal end.* (3) *The immortal soul may exist in an embodied or a disembodied state, preserving all its essential properties in both states.* With these positions in mind, a sketch of a Christian-Buddhist apologetic can now be attempted.

6.4 A CHRISTIAN-BUDDHIST APOLOGETIC ON SELVES AND PERSONS

Since I am now about to engage in apologetics, my voice must change. To this point I have been engaging in apologetics in behalf of a particular thesis, the NOIA thesis, which is itself not a doctrine of many religious communities—perhaps of none in the form offered here. I have been arguing that the representative intellectuals of all religious communities should adopt the NOIA principle as a guide to appropriate behavior in certain contexts. For convenience I restate the principle here:

If representative intellectuals belonging to some specific religious community come to judge at a particular time that some or all of their own doctrine-expressing sentences are incompatible with some alien religious claim(s), then they should feel obliged to engage in both positive and negative apologetics vis-à-vis these alien religious claim(s) and their promulgators.

Since this is a principle intended to be applicable to the representative intellectuals of all religious communities, arguing for it does not require speaking from within the bounds of any particular community. But the NOIA principle itself, if accepted, requires that engagement in apologetics, when it occurs, should be done by the representative intellectuals of some specific religious community, on behalf of its doctrine-expressing sentences, and over against those of some other community. And since, to conclude this study, I want to provide an example of apologetics in action, I can do so only by engaging in that mode of discourse as just such a representative intellectual. I must therefore speak from within some community, and I choose to speak from within the religious community that has shaped me and supports me: that of Anglican Christianity.

It would be self-aggrandizement to claim that I represent the community of Anglican Christians in any sense. I hold no office within that community other than as a baptized and communicating lay member, and it is certainly true that my words would not be recognized by those who do hold such office as possessing any authoritative weight. Nevertheless, this is the only religious community of which I have extended experience as an insider, and therefore the only one from within which I can engage in apologetics. The use of first person pronouns and the like in the remainder of this study carries with it, then, the connotation of a voice speaking from within the bounds of this particular community.

It is possible, I think, to engage in a theoretical apologetic on behalf of a religious community of which one is not a member. Much study and an effort of imaginative empathy would be required to do so, and the results would certainly be of interest and might have significant value in many ways. I do not find it difficult, for example, to imagine constructing an apologetic on behalf of some Buddhist community for the doctrine-expressing sentences set forth in 6.2. But the important difference between that kind of artificial apologetic and the real thing is the issue of what is at stake. In genuine and proper apologetics the apologist has something to gain and something to lose; such engagement is fuelled by and centrally concerned with the pursuit of religiously significant truth. The potential benefits are thus much greater than is the case for artificial apologetics.

In the remainder of this chapter, therefore, I shall sketch the outlines of a possible Christian apologetic vis-à-vis Buddhism on the nature of the human person and the existence of the soul, and shall make some comments as to where the exercise might lead. The sketch given will be preliminary and tentative in the extreme.

First, it is necessary to see whether the sketch of a Buddhist and a Christian position on the human person given in 6.1, 6.2, and 6.3 does engage the NOIA principle: would a representative intellectual of a Christian community assenting to the doctrine-expressing sentences labeled C1-C3 below be required to engage in positive or negative apologetics as a result of becoming aware of some Buddhist community whose representative intellectuals assert the doctrine-expressing sentences labeled B1-B3 below?

(C1) The possession of an immortal soul gives every human person identity.

(C2) The immortal soul is an enduring spiritual substance with a temporal beginning but no temporal end.

(C3) The immortal soul may exist in an embodied or a disembodied state, preserving all its essential properties in both states.

(B1) All personal proper names refer to causally connected continua of events and to nothing else; an exhaustive analysis of the human person may be given in terms of these continua of events.

(B2) Intellectual understanding and personal appropriation of the truth of B1 is a necessary condition for the attainment of Nirvana.

(B3) Assent to any doctrine-expressing sentence contradicting B1 or any entailment thereof will necessarily be productive of suffering.

Using the terminology already established in chapters 1 and 2, the first thing I must do is to see whether there is a prima facie incompatibility between C1-C3 (or any member of that set) and B1-B3 (or any member of that set). It seems evident that there is such an incompatibility between C1 and C2, taken together, and B1. For B1 explicitly claims that a complete descriptive analysis of persons can be given in terms of the five aggregates, the five causally connected continua of events. This claim entails that the referent of any personal proper name must be temporally indexed: it must be the totality of events occurring within a specific collocation of continua at a particular time. This is so because none of the events that occur within any of the continua endures for very long. B1 as it stands gives no very precise answer to the question of how long each event may last; but the central thrust of Buddhist metaphysics is to deny that anything, and so, a fortiori, any event, lasts very long. Many Buddhist metaphysicians assert that all existents are strictly momentary or instantaneous (*yat sat tat kshanikam*), and although this is not a universally agreed position, the emphasis on the impermanence of all existents is universally agreed.

C1 and C2 together are in contradiction with both parts of B1. For C1 entails, assuming an additional premise that personal proper names refer to that which gives persons their identity, that which, among other things, individuates them from other persons, that the referent of any personal proper name is (at least in part) the immortal soul possessed by that person. There is thus a prima facie contradiction on the reference of personal proper names. On the Buddhist view my personal proper name "Paul Griffiths" refers, on any given occasion of its utterance, to the set of momentary events that constitutes the five aggregates which in turn constitute the complete continuum of events that constitutes "me." On the Christian view "Paul Griffiths" refers principally to my immortal soul, a soul that happens at the moment to be embodied, but need not necessarily be so.

Underlying this prima facie contradiction on the referential capacities of personal proper names is a further ontological contradiction: a contradiction concerning what exists in the world. C2 and C3 together make a strong claim that a certain kind of substance both logically can exist and actually does so: souls are understood to be structured enduring entities, possessors of properties, without temporal end, and so forth. Connected with this, of course, though not explicit in any of C1-C3, is a claim about the existence of God as the paradigm case of such a substance; but that claim need not detain us here. While B1-B3 by themselves do not entail (nor, perhaps, do they even suggest) that such substances cannot exist, they certainly do entail that such substances, if they do exist, have nothing to do with human persons, and are never embodied as C3 claims. Further, although this too cannot be properly explored here, Buddhist metaphysics in general is predicated upon a denial of the possibility of the existence of any substance whatsoever; the prima facie contradiction evident here will thus be found to cut very deep indeed if pursued.

Faced, as a Christian intellectual, with B1 and its entailments, I then judge that there is indeed a prima facie incompatibility between C1-C3, which are doctrine-expressing sentences that my community wishes to assert, and B1, a doctrine-expressing sentence of another religious community. The preliminary conditions for the application of the NOIA principle are thus present. Are there other incompatibilities? Let us consider B2. The claim that attaining Nirvana is causally dependent upon assenting to and appropriating B1 is not obviously incompatible with any of C1-C3, though it may be that one of B2's implicit presuppositions is. Underlying B2 is the presupposition that the attainment of Nirvana is desirable: this is an axiological claim, a claim about the value of some goal, and thus also about the value of courses of action that lead to this goal.

How might I, as a Christian intellectual, be able to work out whether this axiological claim stands in contradiction, or tension, with any axiological claims that my community wishes to assert? The first step, obviously, would be to find out what is meant by the attainment of Nirvana. With some preliminary ideas as to what this means, a preliminary judgement on the issue of incompatibility could be made, and, if appropriate, the NOIA principle might be called into action once again.

As a matter of fact it is far from obvious whether the axiological claim underlying B2—the claim that the *attainment of Nirvana is desirable* or some such—does stand in contradiction with any important Christian axiological claim. This is in part because of the exegetical difficulties involved in sorting out what Buddhist communities mean by claims involving Nirvana; but it is also partly because of the difficulty of sorting out the meaning and implications of key Christian axiological claims (such as, for example, *everyone should work to bring about the kingdom of God*). I shall not make any attempt to engage in either exegetical enterprise here. But even without pursuing the possible incompatibility between B2 and its presuppositions and C1-C3, it is worth noticing how suggestive and heuristically valuable the questions being asked here are.

If I, as a Christian intellectual, were to pursue the questions noted in this and the preceding paragraph, I would do so by formulating, on the basis of my reading of Buddhist texts and discussions with members of Buddhist communities, what I think to be suggested by the axiological claim *the attainment of Nirvana is desirable*. This formulation would inevitably involve me in developing some statement or set of such about what Nirvana is. If this statement were then to be tried out upon Buddhists, together with my preliminary arguments as to why the axiological claim in question is not acceptable to Christians, some very interesting results would be likely to follow: refinements and advances in both my understanding of what Nirvana is and (equally important) in the understanding of my Buddhist interlocutors on this matter would be bound to follow. More important, these refinements and developments would follow at a pace and with a passion that it is hard to imagine being produced by any other method. But this particular issue is not one that I am able to pursue further here.

What about B3? Here too there is no prima facie contradiction with anything claimed in C1-C3. But, as was also the case with B2, there may be other reasons why I, as a Christian intellectual, should find it unacceptable. First (and on this set of issues also I shall offer only the most sketchy responses), assent to B3 entails, since I have already established that C1-C3 conjointly contradict B1, that assenting to C1-C3 (as I do), will necessarily be productive of suffering for me. My Buddhist interlocutor will therefore judge that I must suffer because of my adherence to C1-C3.

A short and easy way with this claim is to assent to it also, but to find it no criticism because there is little (perhaps nothing) in Christian doctrine that suggests that suffering should always be avoided, especially when that suffering is in the service of truth. If this short and easy way is taken, it will be evident that any disagreement there is about B3 reduces to disagreement about the truth of B1 and its entailments—and on this I have already suggested that there is genuine and basic disagreement, and I shall return to it in a moment.

But there is also a deeper disagreement here, one that can only be brought out by exploring more fully what is meant by "suffering" in both traditions. Here too I can do no more than point to the issue. For Buddhists, suffering is axiomatically something to be removed. The entire diagnosis of the human condition, sketched briefly in 6.1, stresses this. To suggest that assenting to a particular doctrine-expressing sentence will bring suffering with it is enough by itself to indicate that such assent should not be given.

This is not true for Christians; suffering, in some senses and on some occasions, is to be embraced and welcomed. More even than this, the Buddhist tradition affirms consistently that any and all attachments involving passion must necessarily bring suffering with them. Assent to C1-C3 involves such attachment, since these claims affirm the existence of an entity to which passionate attachment, or at least consistent interest, seems perfectly appropriate.

A full apologetic on this question would have to explore the implications of these disagreements, and would end, inevitably, in analyzing whether and in what sense the love of God is a passionate attachment in the Buddhist sense of those terms. Here also the heuristic benefits are obvious: there appears to be no other way in which I, as an interested Christian, could learn as much as quickly about the Buddhist rejection of attachment and about the views of my own tradition on love as by engaging in this kind of apologetic.

I have indicated that while there are no prima facie contradictions between B2, B3 and C1-C3, there are deeper disagreements, contradictions present in the presuppositions and entailments of both sets of claims. These provide rich material for future apologetical exercises. The explicit contradictions, however, are those between B1 and C1-C3. A few more detailed comments now need to be made on the apologetical possibilities present here; and here again I wish to stress that I speak from within the bounds of a Christian community. On examining B1 I realize that it is incompatible with C1-C3, for the reasons already briefly outlined. Since my membership in a Christian religious community leads me to affirm that C1-C3 are true (which means, naturally, that their entailments and presuppositions are also thought by me to be true), I must regard B1 as it stands, together with its presuppositions and entailments, to be false. If I am to follow the NOIA principle, I must engage in apologetics vis-à-vis B1 and those who assent to it.

In the sketch that follows I shall try to show that B1 is false. Since B1 is a potential defeater of C1-C3, this is best understood as negative apologetics. By showing that B1 is false I shall not offer any arguments in favor of C1-C3, but shall simply remove one potential defeater of them and so defend them against one attack from without. I do not, of course, think that the arguments to follow are final or definitive. They are intended instead to further the debate, and, ideally, to give rise to responses.

The first move is to add to B1 one of its presuppositions, a pan-Buddhist affirmation about the multiplicity of lives undergone by all human persons, and to see how these claims stand together. B1, recall, is:

(B1) All personal proper names refer to causally connected continua of events and to nothing else; an exhaustive analysis of the human person may be given in terms of these continua of events.

Let us add to it:

(B4) Any specific continuum of causally connected events conventionally called a human person does not cease with death.

Affirming the doctrine of rebirth in these terms is meant to point out that the continuity of identity across lives required by the doctrine is merely a causal continuity; any tendency to postulate a more substantial "something" that dies and is reborn is un-Buddhist, because it offends against the no-Self doctrine affirmed in B1. The kind of continuity of identity that occurs across lives is not different in any essential from that which occurs within one life. For any given human person, to say of her that she is "the same person" at two different times means, on the Buddhist view, simply that each momentarily existing state of affairs within the continuum labeled "Jane Doe" is caused by the immediately preceding set of momentary states of affairs within that same continuum, and itself causes the immediately subsequent set within that same continuum. There is no space in the theory for any stronger sense of personal identity, either within or across lives. The Buddhist affirmation of B1 and B4, then, simply says that the nature and extent of personal continuity across many lives is qualitatively no different from the nature and extent of personal continuity within one life.

I begin my apologetic by suggesting that it is difficult to give B1 and B4 together any interesting sense, because it is not clear that any of the criteria that can be used to differentiate one continuum from another (let us say continuum X from continuum Y) in one life can continue to be applied across lives. For example: suppose continuum X has the name "John Smith" in one life; John Smith is differentiated from the other continua with which he interacts during his life by certain obvious criteria. These include physical continuity (he has the same body and not that characteristic of another continuum), continuity of memory (he has the memories that apply to past events within continuum X and not those within continuum Y), continuity of character traits, and so forth. The problem is that none of these differentiating characteristics—those things that make continuum X John Smith, and not, say, Ronald Reagan—may be found in the (postulated) continuation of continuum X in another life. The reborn John Smith does not have the previous John Smith's memories, his body, or his character traits. In what sense, then, is he John Smith?

The standard Buddhist answer to this is that the reborn John Smith is neither the same as nor different from the previous John Smith: he is simply an effect of his predecessor. The continuity is causal. But what kind of causality is at work here? An image often used is that of lighting one candle flame from another and then extinguishing the first. The second candle flame, it is said, relates to the first in the same way that the reborn John Smith relates to the John Smith of a previous life. But suppose we simultaneously light six candles from one original and then extinguish the original. Which is the "proper" continuation, the closest continuer? Do we have six John Smiths?

This should serve at least to illustrate the limitations of argument by analogy, and to point out the main problem underlying this debate. In order to give content to the assertion that a given continuum does not cease with death, the criteria that demarcate the continuum in question from others must be stated. We must know—and be able to say—in what sense continuum X is still continuum X and not continuum Y. For the Buddhist metaphysician this gives rise to an insoluble problem: the precision and fullness with which such criteria of demarcation are stated is in inverse proportion to the compatibility of the resultant view with the standard no-Self doctrine. B1 and B4, while tenable in their bare form, become almost completely without philosophical interest since they are close to being contentless. They end by saying that all events in a given continuum have effects, and that such effects do not cease with the event called death, but they provide no way of determining whether the effect of a given action occurs "within" or "outside" a given continuum, because there are no available criteria to effectively individuate one continuum from another, either within or across lives.

Might Buddhists not simply accept this conclusion and admit that there are no effective ways of individuating continua within or across lives without offending against the no-Self doctrine? This is a difficult option for representatives of the tradition to take, because of its reliance upon ideas about action (*karma*) and its effects upon human beings. Past actions have future effects; morally qualified volitional actions—actions that the agent is free to undertake or not to undertake and which are to be qualified as either positive or negative in terms of Buddhist ethical theory—condition the future of the agent who performed them. And this effect can be (and in some cases must be) transferred across lives: something I do now can have effects upon the nature and extent of one or more of my future lives. Karmic theory, which is dependent upon B4 and its entailments, functions for Buddhists as an explanation of the varied states and conditions of sentient beings. It claims to explain why you are neither a worm nor a Buddha, and why worms are different from both Buddhas and you. It claims to explain why some human persons are born prosperous, healthy, and intelligent, while others are born crippled, deformed, and full of hatred. Karmic theory also grounds Buddhist ideas about moral responsibility: it provides the first-order prescriptions and proscriptions of Buddhist ethics (do not kill, do not steal, do not misbehave yourself sexually, and so forth) with their justification and sanction. If you do engage in such activities, you will suffer for them either in this life or a future one, while if you fulfil your duties (giving to monks, developing compassion, and so forth), you will have a good rebirth. If B1 and B4 are emptied of content in the way that I have suggested, standard-issue karmic theory cannot function in the ways that the tradition requires it to.

This brief set of apologetical arguments is intended, from a Christian viewpoint, to remove the effect of B1 and B4 as potential defeators of C1-C3. It has suggested that B1 and B4 are significantly weakened by their incapacity to provide criteria for individuating continua from one another without falling into incoherence; and by their further inability to accept this incapacity as a result of the imperative under which the tradition has placed itself to provide some conceptual account of the location of moral responsibility in persons, both within and across lives. More briefly: the Buddhist rejection of souls fails; without some strong criterion of individuation an adequate account of the continuity of personal identity cannot be given, and without such an account, needs that the Buddhist tradition itself recognizes cannot be met.

Where might the apologetic go from here? There are two major directions. The first, to be constructed by Buddhist thinkers for their own tradition, is a negative apologetic on behalf of B1 and B4 against the criticisms offered here. Such an apologetic would try to show that B1 and B4 can be given sufficient conceptual content to perform the tasks that the Buddhist tradition requires of them, without falling into incoherence. This would presumably be done by pursuing the notion of causal continuity as a guarantor of continuity of personal identity, and by elaborating the notions of causation implicit in such a task. There is much material within the Buddhist tradition on this.

Secondly, representative intellectuals of Buddhist communities would presumably wish to engage in apologetics against C1-C3. The principal way of doing this would be to construct arguments purporting to show that the Christian idea of the soul is incoherent, or that there is not sufficient evidence to affirm its existence. And there is also a great deal in the way of intellectual resources within the Buddhist traditions for engagement in such an enterprise. Once again, the potential heuristic benefits here are enormous, and I hope that the apologetical debates sketched in this chapter will come to form a major part of the interaction between Buddhists and Christians in the future.

I hope it is evident, from this brief discussion, that my expectations in undertaking this sketch for an apologetic are not simply of victory and vindication. Naturally, I think that I and my community are right to believe what we believe. I must also therefore necessarily think that when it appears to me that Buddhists assert something that stands in direct contradiction to what I hold, they must be wrong. But—and this is important—the fact that I do not hold C1-C3 to be beyond revision, and that I therefore do not hold assent to them to be a necessary component of Christian orthodoxy, means that I can see possibilities for revision in them suggested by the apologetical engagement with B1-B3. I can also see possibilities for a broader Buddhist enrichment of my Christian understanding of the processes by which the experienced facts of self-identity come to occur. Appropriation and creative borrowing are just as important as engagement in positive and negative apologetics; neither need exclude the other, just as long as both are taken with intellectual seriousness and argumentative passion.

Bibliography

The bibliographical suggestions made here are keyed to the chapter- and section-divisions of the main text. They note only those works that have been of major importance for this study. In no case do I attempt to provide complete documentation for any of the issues discussed.

1. THE NECESSITY OF INTERRELIGIOUS APOLOGETICS

A richly documented and well written historical survey of apologetics as an intellectual discipline within the catholic tradition, of considerable use for the comments made in this chapter, is Avery Dulles's *A History of Apologetics* (Philadelphia: Westminster Press, 1971).

1.1 I published an earlier formulation and defense of the NOIA principle in an article entitled "An Apology for Apologetics" (*Faith and Philosophy* 5/4 [1988] pp. 399–420).

1.2 The work of Wilfred Cantwell Smith on the improper reification of religious traditions is important for the discussion of religious communities contained in 1.2. See especially *The Meaning and End of Religion: A New Approach to the Religious Traditions of Mankind* (New York: Macmillan, 1963); *Belief and History* (Charlottesville: University of Virginia Press, 1977); *Faith and Belief* (Princeton, New Jersey: Princeton University Press, 1979); and *Towards a World Theology* (Philadelphia: Westminster Press, 1981). Important for the discussion of the function of intellectuals within religious communities is William A Christian, Sr.'s work, especially *Oppositions of Religious Doctrines* (London and New York: Macmillan, 1972) and *Doctrines of Religious Communities* (New Haven: Yale University Press, 1987).

1.3 The term "doctrine-expressing sentences" is borrowed from William A. Christian, Sr., and much of the discussion in this and the immediately following sections is heavily dependent upon his work.

1.4 See, again, Christian's *Oppositions of Religious Doctrines* and *Doctrines of Religious Communities.*

1.5 For some of these ideas about apologetics I am indebted to discussions with Phil Quinn. For a splendid dialogical exploration of the differences between positive and negative apologetics, see Gary Gutting's "The Catholic and the Calvinist: A Dialogue on Faith and Reason" (*Faith and Philosophy* 2 [1985] pp. 236–56). For a good example of the Tibetan *Grub mtha'* texts mentioned in this section, see 'Jigs med dbang po's *Grub pa'i mtha'i rnam bzhag rin po che'i phreng ba,* easily available in English translation. See H.V. Guenther, *Buddhist Philosophy in Theory and Practice* (Berkeley: Shambhala Press, 1971), and Geshe Lhundup Sopa and Jeffrey Hopkins, *Practice and Theory of Tibetan Buddhism*

(London: Rider, 1976). The intellectual systems discussed in such texts are straw men, not real debating partners.

2. THE PROPERTIES OF DOCTRINE-EXPRESSING SENTENCES

2.1 For the Derridean version of the worries about meaning and understanding see Jacques Derrida, *Of Grammatology*, translated by Gayatri Chakravorty Spivak (Baltimore: Johns Hopkins Press, 1977); *Writing and Difference*, translated by Alan Bass (London: Routledge & Kegan Paul, 1978); *Limited Inc*, translated by Samuel Weber and Jeffrey Mehlman (Evanston, Illinois: Northwestern University Press, 1988). This last is especially useful for Derrida's comments on speech-act theory. See also Roland Barthes, *Elements of Semiology*, translated by Annette Lavers and Colin Smith (London: Jonathan Cape, 1967); *S/Z*, translated by Richard Miller (London: Jonathan Cape, 1975). For the Quinean version see especially the essays collected in W.V.O. Quine, *Word and Object* (Cambridge, Massachusetts: MIT Press, 1960).

2.2 The thought of Ramanuja, taken as an example of commensurability in this section, is made available in John B. Carman, *The Theology of Ramanuja* (New Haven, Connecticut: Yale University Press, 1974); J.A.B. Van Buitenen, *Ramanuja on the Bhagavadgita: A Condensed Rendering of the Gitabhashya with Copious Notes and an Introduction* (Delhi: Motilal Banarsidass, 1974); Julius Lipner, *The Face of Truth: A Study of Meaning and Metaphysics in the Vedantic Theology of Ramanuja* (Albany: State University of New York Press, 1986). On the history of Indian logic and its commensurability with Western thought, see especially the work of Frits Staal, a convenient recent collection of which may be found in Staal, *Universals: Studies in Indian Logic and Linguistics* (Chicago and London: University of Chicago Press, 1988). And on the whole question of Christian-Muslim contacts and images of one another in the medieval period, see R.W. Southern, *Western Views of Islam in the Middle Ages* (Cambridge: Cambridge University Press, 1962); Norman Daniel, *Islam and the West: The Making of an Image* (Edinburgh: Edinburgh University Press, 1960).

2.1 Useful background on the question of conceptual relativism may be found in Martin Hollis and Steven Lukes, eds., *Rationality and Relativism* (Oxford: Blackwell, 1982); Michael Krausz and Jack W. Meiland, eds., *Relativism: Cognitive and Moral* (Notre Dame and London: University of Notre Dame Press, 1982); and Michael Krausz, *Relativism: Interpretation and Confrontation* (Notre Dame and London: University of Notre Dame Press, 1989). The equivalence principle enunciated and discussed in this section is modeled after one stated by Barry Barnes and David Bloor in "Relativism, Rationalism and the Sociology of Knowledge," in Martin Hollis and Steven Lukes, eds., *Rationality and Relativism* (Oxford: Basil Blackwell, 1982), pp. 21–47.

2.2 For the term "experiential expressivism" and for much of the discussion 2.2 I am indebted to George Lindbeck's *The Nature of Doctrine: Religion and Theology in a Postliberal Age* (Philadelphia: Westminster Press, 1984).

2.3 Once again, my central debt here is to Lindbeck's *Nature of Doctrine*. Even though I cannot agree with the line taken by Lindbeck in his defense of a rule theory of religious doctrines, his discussion is very stimulating. On performative utterances, discussed in the context of criticising a rule-theoretical interpretation of religious doctrines, see, classically, J.L. Austin, "Performative Utterances," in Austin, *Philosophical Papers* (Oxford: Clarendon Press, 1961), pp. 220–39.

3. INCOMPATIBILITY AMONG DOCTRINE-EXPRESSING SENTENCES

3.1 On the kind of universalist perspectivalism discussed in here, the most important current works are by John Hick, a British theologian who is currently the Danforth Professor of Religion at the Claremont Graduate School in California. And it is mostly his thought that I have in mind here. His most recent large work is *An Interpretation of Religion* (New Haven: Yale University Press, 1988). A classic statement of his position is in "Whatever Path Men Choose is Mine," in John Hick and Brian Hebblethwaite, eds., *Christianity and Other Religions* (Glasgow: Collins, 1980), pp. 171–90. A useful collection of Hick's many essays is *Problems of Religious Pluralism* (New York: St. Martin's Press, 1985), and a good collection of discussions of Hick's work is to be found in a special number of *Faith and Philosophy* (54, October 1988) on religious pluralism, together with Hick's replies thereto. The lengthy quotation beginning "The great world faiths," is taken from Hick, "Religious Pluralism and Absolute Claims," in Leroy S. Rouner, ed., *Religious Pluralism* (Notre Dame: University of Notre Dame Press, 1984), p. 194. The phrase "the fruits of openness to the divine Reality are gloriously apparent" is also Hick's: "On Conflicting Religious Truth-Claims," *Religious Studies* 19 (1983) p. 488.

3.2 A classic exposition of esotericist perspectivalism may be found in Aldous Huxley's *The Perennial Philosophy* (London: Chatto & Windus, 1972; first published 1946). A more recent version is in Seyyed Hossein Nasr, *Knowledge and the Sacred* (New York: Crossroad, 1981). The lengthy quotation beginning "Philosophia perennis," is from Huxley, *The Perennial Philosophy*, p. 1.

3.1 I am indebted here to—though in various ways I disagree with—R.C. Zaehner's work, especially *Mysticism Sacred and Profane* (New York and London: Oxford University Press, 1961). See also William J. Wainwright, *Mysticism: A Study of its Nature, Cognitive Value and Moral Implications* (Wisconsin: University of Wisconsin Press, 1981), and especially Steven Katz, ed., *Mysticism and Philosophical Analysis* (New York: Oxford University Press, 1978). A lineal ancestor of the remarks made in this section and the next appeared as Paul J. Griffiths & Delmas Lewis, "Wainwright on Mysticism" (*Religious Studies* 20 [1984] pp. 293–304). More recently, see Robert K. C. Forman, ed., *The Problem of Pure Consciousness: Mysticism and Philosophy* (New York: Oxford University Press, 1990), and my essay therein (71–97) on "Pure Consciousness and Indian Buddhism."

4. THE REJECTION OF POSITIVE APOLOGETICS

4.1 The argument from negative effect is explicit in many of Hick's works—for which see the bibliographical annotations to chapter 3—and is implicit in perhaps the majority of recent works on interreligious dialogue. The lengthy quotation beginning "Among spiritual faiths" is taken from Tenzin Gyatso [Dalai Lama XIV], *Kindness, Clarity, and Insight* (Ithaca, New York: Snow Lion, 1984), pp. 45, 47. On *upayakaushalya*, presented in this section as a partial Buddhist version of the argument from negative effect, see Michael Pye *Skillful Means* (London: Duckworth, 1978).

4.2–4.5 The arguments offered in these sections are intended to engage some implications of the currently fashionable religious epistemology put forward by, most importantly, Alvin Plantinga. See, for example, Plantinga, "Advice to Christian Philosophers" (*Faith and Philosophy* 1 [1984] 253–71); "On Reformed Epistemology" (*The Reformed Journal* 32/1 [January 1982] 13–17); "Reformed Epistemology Again" (*The Reformed Journal* 32/7 [July 1982] 7–8); "The Reformed Objection to Natural Theology" (*Proceedings of the American Catholic Philosophical Association* [1980] 49–64); "Reason and Belief in God" (in Alvin Plantinga and Nicholas Wolterstorff, eds., *Faith and Rationality: Reason and Belief in God* [Notre Dame, Indiana: University of Notre Dame Press, 1983] 16–93). The quotation in 4.3.1 beginning "Indeed on the Pumpkinite tradition" is taken from Plantinga's "On Reformed Epistemology," 14. The original reads "God" where I have substituted "the Great Pumpkin" and "Reformed tradition" for my "Pumpkinite tradition."

5. PROPER APOLOGETICS

5.1 One example of an apologetical engagement in an inappropriate political context was that between British Christian missionaries and traditionally trained Indian pandits in the 1840s. Some of this has been chronicled by Richard F. Young in *Resistant Hinduism: Sanskrit Sources on Anti-Christian Apologetics in Early Nineteenth-Century India* (Publications of the De Nobili Research Library, vol. 8; Vienna: De Nobili Research Library, 1981). Inappropriate though the context was, this particular apologetical engagement was not entirely without benefit to both sides.

6. APOLOGETICS IN ACTION

6.1 A useful and relatively accessible text giving a classical Indian Buddhist refutation of the existence of the Self is Vasubandhu's *Refutation of the Person (pudgalapratishedha)*. This short work is an appendix (or ninth chapter) to the large scholastic compendium by this author entitled *Treasury of Metaphysics (Abhidharmakosha)*. A complete French translation is available: Louis de La Vallée Poussin (trs.), *L'Abhidharmakoça de Vasubandhu* (in six volumes; Paris: Paul Geuthner, 1923–31; reprinted in *Mélanges chinois et bouddhiques* 16 [1971]). An English translation of this is available. See Leo Pruden (trs.), *Abhidharmakoshabhashyam* (Berkeley: Asian Humanities Press, 1988–90). Two English translations of the appendix or ninth chapter are: T. Stcherbatsky, *Soul Theory of the Buddhists* (Delhi: Bharatiya Vidya Prakashan, 1976), and Matthew Kapstein, "Self and Personal Identity in Indian Buddhist Scholasticism: A Philosophical Investigation" (Ph.D dissertation, Brown University, 1987), 242–72. The latter is much the more reliable. The lengthy extract giving the simile of the chariot in Nagasen's reply to Milinda is taken from I. B. Horner (trs.), *Milinda's Questions* (London: Pali Text Society, 1963–64), 1:37.

6.2 The best single secondary source on the Buddhist description of the person is Steven Collins's *Selfless Persons: Imagery and Thought in Theravada Buddhism* (Cambridge: Cambridge University Press, 1982). See also, for a brief and simple account, Walpola Rahula, *What the Buddha Taught* (second edition; Bedford, England: Gordon Fraser, 1967).

6.3 I am indebted for much of what is said in this section to Richard Swinburne's work, especially *The Evolution of the Soul* (Oxford: Clarendon Press, 1986), and

"The Structure of the Soul" (in Arthur Peacocke and Grant Gillett, eds., *Persons & Personality: A Contemporary Inquiry* [Oxford: Blackwell, 1987] 33–55). The quotation from Aristotle on memory is taken from Richard Sorabji (trs.), *Aristotle on Memory* (London: Duckworth, 1972), p. 48.

6.4 The preliminary and sketchy Buddhist-Christian apologetic given here develops some of the ideas found in my exchange with J. C. White. See Paul J. Griffiths, "Notes Towards A Critique of Buddhist Karmic Theory" (*Religious Studies* 18 [1982] 277–91); J. C. White, "Is Karmic Theory False?" (*Religious Studies* 19 [1983] 223–28); Paul J. Griffiths, "Karma and Personal Identity: A Response to Professor White" (*Religious Studies* 20 [1984] 481–85). See also some of the points on the mind-body relation made in my *On Being Mindless: Buddhist Meditation and the Mind-Body Problem* (La Salle, Illinois: Open Court, 1986).